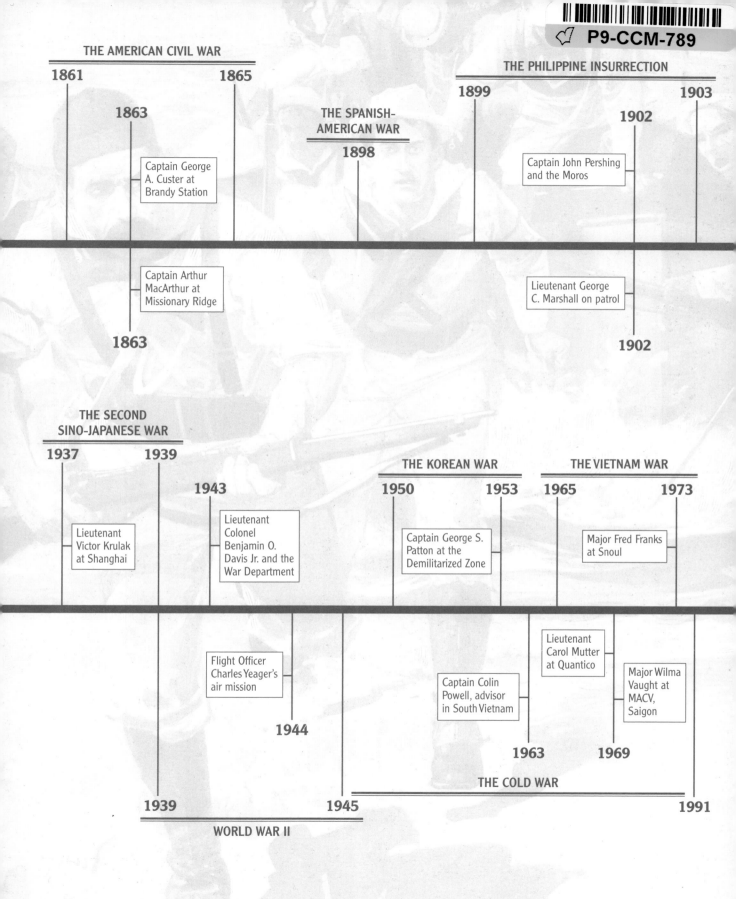

THE AMERICAN CIVIL WAR

1861   1865

1863

Captain George
A. Custer at
Brandy Station

THE PHILIPPINE INSURRECTION

1899   1903

1902

Captain John Pershing
and the Moros

THE SPANISH-
AMERICAN WAR

1898

Captain Arthur
MacArthur at
Missionary Ridge

1863

Lieutenant George
C. Marshall on patrol

1902

THE SECOND
SINO-JAPANESE WAR

1937   1939

1943

Lieutenant
Victor Krulak
at Shanghai

Lieutenant
Colonel
Benjamin O.
Davis Jr. and the
War Department

THE KOREAN WAR

1950   1953

Captain George S.
Patton at the
Demilitarized Zone

THE VIETNAM WAR

1965   1973

Major Fred Franks
at Snoul

Flight Officer
Charles Yeager's
air mission

1944

Lieutenant
Carol Mutter
at Quantico

Major Wilma
Vaught at
MACV,
Saigon

Captain Colin
Powell, advisor
in South Vietnam

1963   1969

THE COLD WAR

1939   1945   1991

WORLD WAR II

FIRST COMMAND

Paths to Leadership

DWIGHT JON ZIMMERMAN

Foreword by James M. McPherson

VANDAMERE
PRESS

DEDICATION

To my "commanding generals," Joëlle, Eric, and Léa

To Joe—
A history buff. Hope
you enjoy the stories!
Dwight Jon Zimmerman

Published by
Vandamere Press
P.O. Box 149
St. Petersburg, FL 33731
USA

Copyright 2005
by Dwight Jon Zimmerman

ISBN 0-918339-62-6

CONTENTS

FOREWORD

Did you ever wonder how famous and successful people got their start? Like the rest of us, they were once children, then teenagers, then young adults. Many of them were unremarkable in their early years. But as they matured, something special happened—an opportunity, a challenge, an obstacle to overcome. They met the challenge in a manner that gave promise of future greatness. They were on their way.

The challenge of war is the toughest one of all. War brings out both the worst and best in people. It presents the literal issue of life and death. From the French and Indian War in the eighteenth century to the Persian Gulf War in the twenty-first century, America has fought many wars. Each of them brought forth young soldiers or officers who performed exceptional deeds that promised future greatness. This splendid book tells the stories of 23 such soldiers and Marines. All of them demonstrated courage, initiative, and striking qualities of leadership as young men or women in one war. Subsequently, they became generals who held important commands in a later war. Their stories are dramatic and inspirational.

The armed forces of the United States are the most racially and ethnically integrated institutions in American society. Promotion is based not on who you are but what you have done and can do. African-Americans, Hispanics, Jews, and anyone else—including in recent decades women—can rise to the top. It wasn't always that way. One of the themes of these 23 biographies is the opening of the armed forces to previously excluded or marginalized groups.

For each man or woman whose career is described in this book, Dwight Jon Zimmerman chronicles a wartime experience of the young soldier or Marine that started him or her up the ladder of success. The reader will come away with admiration for these remarkable individuals and greater understanding of America's wars. I commend *First Command* to readers of all ages.

—*James M. McPherson*

ACKNOWLEDGMENTS

This is my opportunity to thank the many people and institutions who helped me. For some, this meant graciously allowing me to interview them, for others it was a willingness to advise. To these people and everyone else who gave me their support at key moments, and to the historians and biographers whose works were invaluable, I am deeply grateful.

I especially wish to thank (in alphabetical order) Brig. General Clara Adams-Ender, U.S. Army (Ret.), Judith Bellafaire, Martin Blumenson, Philip Caputo, Marilla Cushman, Dr. John Ferling, Dr. Sholly Fisch, John Gresham, Gary Grossman, Maj. General Jeanne Holm, U.S. Air Force, (Ret.), New York State Senator Seymour Lachman, the Library of Congress, James M. McPherson, Lt. General Carol Mutter, the National Archives, Steven Ossad, Kelly Smith, Craig Symonds, Dennis Trott, Brig. General Wilma Vaught, U.S. Air Force, (Ret.), the Women in Military Service for America Memorial Foundation, Brig. General Chuck Yeager, U.S. Air Force (Ret.), my brother Christian Zimmerman, Mary Fox Zimmerman, and the individuals listed in the bibliography. Also, though they made no direct contribution to this book, I would be remiss if I did not thank David Anthony Kraft who many years ago gave me my first writing opportunity and Byron Preiss who gave me the chance to achieve a second dream, that of writing military history. I am deeply grateful to my publisher, Art Brown, of Vandamere Press for his insight and support. And finally, I thank my wife, Joëlle, my son, Eric, and daughter, Léa, who put up with a husband and father in his long journey through this manuscript. As for any errors or omissions, they are solely my responsibility.

INTRODUCTION

Wars are fought by armies, but an army without an effective leader is little more than an armed mob in fancy dress. Those leaders in high command who wear the uniforms of the Army, Marine Corps, and Air Force—the generals—are a different breed of people. They have to be. Achieving "star" rank and at the pinnacle of their careers, these individuals possess the power of life and death over their fellow man. They are also aware that their success or failure in battle can, for good or ill, affect the fortune of their nation and change the course of history. Throughout America's history there have been men—and most recently, women—able to accept this awesome responsibility, lead troops, and fight the good fight. Thus, though armies battled in the campaigns, it is more often stated that General George Washington won at Yorktown in 1781; that General Robert E. Lee won at Chancellorsville and lost at Gettysburg in 1863; that General Ulysses S. Grant won at Vicksburg in the same year; and that General Dwight Eisenhower was the victor in Europe in 1945.

My fascination with generals and their battles began when I was young. My father was in the Seventh Army in World War II and served, distantly, under Dwight Eisenhower. Originally, my father wanted to name me after the man who saved his life in the war, but for reasons never quite explained, instead of becoming "Sam Zimmerman," I was named "Dwight," and thus became another of many veterans' sons christened with Eisenhower's first name. I had a typical small town upbringing in that period before Gameboys, Play Stations, and Xboxes, which is to say I was outside when the weather was fair, and sometimes when it wasn't. It was a young life full of adventure, sometimes real but more often imagined. I also loved to read. I regularly visited the library, usually selecting the maximum permitted number of five books. Some were fiction, but most were histories and biographies—particularly military history. For the two weeks that these books were mine, I "marched to the sound of guns" and smelled the "whiff of grapeshot" as I avidly read the accounts of American generals and their battles. I cannot say that I was the most regular young visitor to the Carnegie Public Library of Devils Lake, North Dakota. But at a time when library cards were made of paper and had to be stamped, I went through quite a few blue cards.

The generals became my heroes. It was only much later that I started asking myself what it was like for generals at the beginning of their career—when they had nothing to fall back on but a belief in themselves. Where did they learn the skills they would need? And when did they learn them? Did they make mistakes (of course they must have, but what were they)? How did they overcome them? My search for answers to these and other questions became the basis for this book. I found myself surprised at some of the things I discovered. Some generals, including John Pershing, George Marshall, George S. Patton, Jr., and Lewis "Chesty" Puller, gained experience on now-forgotten battlefields in obscure wars, where they learned the art of command. They led troops, both educated and illiterate, and composed of everything from citizen and career soldiers to foreigners and headhunters, against Muslims, guerillas, and bandits. Others, including Maurice Rose and Charles "Chuck" Yeager, gained experience in some of the most famous conflicts in American history. Still others, such as Dwight Eisenhower and Elwood "Pete" Quesada, gained experience without ever hearing the sound of a gun fired in anger.

There were challenges faced by sons who chose to pursue the same career path as their successful fathers. Douglas MacArthur had a father who had won the Medal of Honor in the American Civil War and had reached the rank of lieutenant general, the highest rank possible in the army at the turn of the twentieth century. George Patton and Benjamin O. Davis, Jr., were namesakes. Davis had the additional hurdle of racial discrimination.

First commands are rightly assumed to occur when one is a junior officer—a lieutenant or captain. But George Washington's first command was as a lieutenant colonel in the Virginia militia. Winfield Scott—a noncommissioned officer—was a lance corporal in the Virginia militia when he had his first command, one that earned him national fame, brought an unprepared country to the brink of war, and resulted in a presidential reprimand.

The ultimate test of military leadership is command in combat. For many years this role of command was denied to women in the military. The only openly acceptable career path for women was in nursing. Until 1967, women were legally barred from rank higher than colonel. Lieutenant General Mutter, the first woman in the Marine Corps to reach three-star rank; and Air Force Brigadier General Wilma Vaught, the first woman comptroller to become a general; were among the group of trailblazers who opened more careers for women in the military. Of women's changing roles and expectations, Mutter recently observed, "I think the women now expect more of the Corps and from their time in the Corps than we did because we knew there were limitations and we accepted those and worked within those. There are very few restrictions now and more is expected of them and they expect to do more."

Thomas Jackson faced enormous obstacles in his life. He was largely self-taught and an orphan when he entered the U.S. Military Academy at West Point as a member of the class of 1846. Had "Stonewall" remained in the Union, it is easy to imagine that he would have become a Civil War general clad in blue instead of gray. One of Jackson's favorite axioms was, "You may be what ever you resolve to be." What follows are the stories of those who resolved, sometimes against extraordinary challenges, and became what they wanted to be.

—*Dwight Jon Zimmerman*

1

GROWING PAINS

1755~1812

 **THE FRENCH AND INDIAN WAR**

The three most powerful nations in the eighteenth century were France, England, and Spain. Their rivalry caused many disagreements. Some were settled peacefully, but inevitably some resulted in wars declared both in Europe and in their respective colonies in North America. The vast scale of the largely unexplored North American continent, the seemingly endless wealth of natural resources, and an expanding colonial population made it inevitable that the struggle for power in Europe would be reflected by these nations' colonies in the New World. The series of off-and-on conflicts on the North American continent among these three European powers lasted almost a hundred years. Collectively, these conflicts were called the French and Indian Wars, the last of the conflicts would take the name French and Indian War.

Spain's possessions were the most extensive, covering most of South America, all of Central America, most of the Caribbean islands, Mexico, Florida, and southwestern North America, roughly from what is now Texas to California. France's colonies were primarily in North America: New France (Canada), and, roughly, the Mississippi and Ohio Rivers and their tributaries down to New Orleans. England had the smallest colonial presence: the coastal strip between the Appalachian mountains and the Atlantic Ocean that was home to the thirteen colonies.

The axiom, "possession is nine-tenths of the law," was commonly practiced during the colonial period regarding the wilderness, which at the time was most of North America. An explorer's metal plate marker placed at prominent locations, such as river junctions or a prominent hill or cliff, stating a patron nation's ownership of the region was not enough to ensure that the claim would be respected by rival nations.

The first conflict in the French and Indian Wars began in 1689 with an eight-year struggle called King William's War (between England and France). This was followed by a truce of five years that ended with an eleven-year-long struggle beginning in 1702 called Queen Anne's War (between England, France, and Spain). It was followed by an uneasy peace that lasted for twenty-six years. It ended in a brief flare-up known as the War of Jenkin's Ear in 1739 (between England and Spain) caused by Spanish mistreatment of English merchants and seamen. The war got its name when the Spanish authorities' cut off of the ear of seaman Robert Jenkins. Next came King George's War (involving all three nations and lasting from 1744 to1748), which was the name for the North American side of a larger power struggle between the ruling royal dynasties in Europe that was called the War of Austrian Succession. The last, and largest, of these conflicts in North America was simply called the French and Indian War (between England and France). It began in 1755 and concluded in 1763. It left England in possession of approximately half the North American continent.

The outright struggle for colonial power in North America among the three European powers effectively ended in 1763. As events would show, however, it wasn't really finished. England's domination in North America would last only twenty years. When the thirteen colonies rose in rebellion against England in the American Revolution in 1775, France and Spain stepped in to help the patriots' cause. Their aid helped secure American independence in 1783.

 ## THE WAR OF 1812

The War of 1812 is sometimes called America's "Second War of Independence" because America fought the British less than thirty years after it had won its independence from that country. It occurred because Great Britain refused to recognize the rights of the young United States and because some Americans living in the South and West thought the United States could take Canada away from England and use it as a bargaining chip to force England to respect their rights.

After the signing of the Treaty of Paris of 1783 that ended the American Revolution, the

United States reduced its army and navy to a token force. Large armies and navies are expensive to support. Because the United States was not surrounded by hostile nations as were the countries in Europe, Americans felt that they could survive with just a small military force.

That belief was challenged when the Napoleonic Wars in Europe began in 1800. The United States declared itself neutral from this conflict that involved France under Emperor Napoleon I fighting Great Britain and its allies. At first, the United States benefited from the war. In 1803 Napoleon sold what was called the Louisiana Purchase to the United States because he needed money to finance his war. This doubled the size of the young United States, but it also added to the country's problems with Britain.

The westward expansion of the United States brought explorers and settlers into conflict with Canadians along the northern border. The Treaty of Paris had never settled the exact boundary between Canada and the United States. At the same time, the British navy was claiming that crewmen from their ships were deserting and signing on with crews from neutral nations, particularly the United States, in order to avoid service in the war.

In 1805, British warships, under orders from their government, began intercepting any vessel they suspected of carrying deserters. They sent armed crews to board, search, seize and impress any deserters they found. This impressment policy outraged the American people. They felt it was a violation of their rights to freely travel the seas. The U.S. government protested through diplomatic channels, but because it could not back up these protests with a strong military presence, the British government ignored them. The impressment of sailors, some of them American citizens wrongly taken, continued.

The situation finally reached a breaking point on June 1, 1812, when President James Madison presented Congress with a list of "the spectacle of injuries and indignities which have been heaped on our country [by Great Britain]." On June 18, 1812, the United States declared war. It ended on December 24, 1814, with neither side able to claim a clear-cut victory. After that, however, Britain never attempted to impress American sailors and began to respect America's rights as a nation.

Winfield Scott was one of many young men proud of his new country and outraged by Britain's high-handed actions of impressment in the years leading up to war. One of the most infamous of those actions was the attack of the USS *Chesapeake* by the HMS *Leopard* just off the shores of Virginia in 1807. In the patriotic fervor that resulted, Scott enlisted in the Virginia militia and was given the rank of lance corporal. His successful action in the following account would make him a national hero. While his attack launched the career of one of the most celebrated generals of the nineteenth century, it almost caused the War of 1812 to begin in 1807.

GEORGE WASHINGTON *Starts a War with the Jumonville Affair*

Biography in Brief

GEORGE WASHINGTON (1732-1799), the first President of the United States, began his career as a major in the Virginia militia prior to the French and Indian War. He fought numerous battles in that conflict eventually rising to the rank of honorary brigadier general.

Following the end of the French and Indian War, he entered Virginia politics. He was a delegate from Virginia in the First Continental Congress and a member of the Second Continental Congress. During the War for Independence, also called the American Revolution, Congress appointed him general. As commander of the Continental Army, he successfully conducted the military campaign that defeated the British, retiring shortly after its conclusion with the rank of lieutenant general.

Washington was unanimously elected the first President of the United States in 1789. After serving two terms, he retired to his home in Mt. Vernon, Virginia where he died in 1799. On October 11, 1976, a Joint Resolution of Congress authorized the posthumous appointment of George Washington to the rank of General of the Armies. The following account describes a dramatic moment in his service in the Virginia militia.

It's not often that one individual causes an incident that ignites a world war. Certainly that was not twenty-two-year-old Lieutenant Colonel George Washington's intent when he and his troops from the English colony of Virginia fought a French force in the wilderness of the Ohio River Valley in the spring of 1754. The skirmish was later called the Jumonville Affair after the French commander, Joseph Coulon, Sieur de Jumonville, one of ten Frenchmen killed in the incident.

The man who helped cause such an awesome shift of power was a young, ambitious, self-educated member of colonial Virginia gentry. Though not wealthy in coin, George Washington was rich in family name, land, proper manners, and political connections. By 1753, he had made a rising name for himself in Virginia. Largely through political connections, he began his military career as a major in the Virginia militia and was soon promoted to lieutenant colonel despite having almost no military experience.

In 1753, Robert Dinwiddie, the royal governor of Virginia and Washington's patron, learned that the French were building forts in the upper Ohio River Valley, territory that had been claimed by England. He sent then-Major Washington on a diplomatic mission authorized by Parliament in England to the new French forts with orders to deliver a letter informing the French that they were trespassing and that they should peacefully leave. If they refused, they would be kicked out by force. Though successful in delivering the letter, Washington's mission was a failure. Not only did the French stay they began building additional forts.

On March 15, 1754, Governor Dinwiddie ordered the newly promoted Lt. Colonel Washington "to march what soldiers you have . . . immediately to the Ohio." Once there he was to reassert English authority in the region, "but in case any attempts are made to obstruct . . . or interrupt our settlements by any persons whatsoever, you are to restrain all such offenders and in case of resistance to make prisoners of, or kill and destroy them." Thus did Dinwiddie set the stage for a pivotal

This engraving shows George Washington wearing the uniform of a lieutenant colonel in the Virginia militia during the French and Indian War. The original portrait was painted by Charles Willson Peale in 1772 and is the earliest known portrait of Washington.
(Author's Collection)

event in American history that would redraw the map of the world and for the first time put the name George Washington on the world stage.

Lt. Colonel Washington was energetic and cheerful when on April 18, 1754, he set out from Wills Creek, Virginia, with 159 men, some wagons and cannon for the British settlement of the Forks of the Ohio, almost 200 miles away. Built where Pittsburgh now stands, the "Forks," as it was commonly named, was a small settlement with a half-built fort that was

Washington crosses the Allegheny River on a raft. This engraving is an artist's interpretation of an event that occurred during Washington's first diplomatic mission in the region. Washington was ordered to deliver an official letter to the French, ordering them to leave the area which was claimed by Great Britain. Because Washington arrived without troops, the French refused. (Author's Collection)

GARRISON: Troops inhabiting a military fort or post

threatened by encroaching French forces. Washington's orders were to reinforce the small garrison there. The simplicity of his instructions was hampered by the complexity of the problems he faced in getting there. No road existed through the Allegheny Mountains. If they were going to get their supply wagons and cannon to the Forks, they would have to build one. With ax, saw, shovel, rope, and the strength of their arms, backs, legs, and the muscles of horse and oxen, Washington's men cut, carved, and cleared the way ahead. What his men created was more a long trail than a road. It was barely wide enough for the wagons, and it was dotted in its center with uncleared stumps and boulders. Only the deepest holes were filled in, and the steepest grades somewhat smoothed. This rough roadwork resulted in progress of only two to four miles a day. At that rate, it would take the force almost two months to reach the Forks—and that's if the weather stayed fair and everything proceeded smoothly.

An artist's conception of Washington's retreat from Fort Duquesne in 1755. General Edward Braddock led a British army that included Washington and the Virginia Militia on an attack of the French fort. The assault ended in disaster. Braddock was killed and Washington led his men back in a humiliating retreat. (U.S. Army)

Which, of course, it didn't. Not long after his trek had begun, Washington was surprised to be met by about 30 men coming from the other direction—the garrison of the Forks. They told Washington that more than 60 French bateaux—boats—and 300 canoes carrying "more than a thousand French" troops and 18 cannon had paddled down the Allegheny River and landed near the settlement. The French commander notified the small group at the fort that if they wished to leave, they could do so unharmed. If they refused, they would be attacked. As the men faced trained soldiers and were overwhelmingly outnumbered, it was an offer quickly accepted.

Though the news that the fort was now in enemy hands and renamed Fort Duquesne was distressing, the garrison had additional information that held out some hope for Washington. Both France and England had made alliances with Indian tribes on whose lands they had explored. Both countries learned that such alliances were not always reliable, but they were necessary. Without them, any exploration or settlements in the wilderness was impossible. It was a British alliance with Half-King, a chief of the powerful Seneca tribe, whom Washington had met on his previous expedition to the Ohio, that now proved useful. The men from the garrison told Washington that Half-King had witnessed the French landing

ALLIANCE: A formal agreement of military and/or diplomatic assistance between nations or groups

7

Washington (center) salutes the British flag being raised over Fort Duquensne. In 1758 Washington command-
ed one of three brigades that finally succeeded in conquering the fort. The fort would be renamed Fort Pitt in
honor of British Prime Minister William Pitt. (Author's Collection)

at the Forks and had defiantly threatened the French, stating that he would assist the approaching British army in throwing the French troops out. In the garrison's group were two of Half-King's men who now stared at Washington with interest. Washington had to make a decision. He was outnumbered. (He had no way of knowing that the actual enemy total was about 600 men, still a superior force.) And they were established behind fortifications. But the British alliance with Half-King's tribe, as well as other tribes in the region, was crucial. If Washington didn't arrive at the Forks with his men and make good Half-King's bluster, that alliance would be jeopardized. This was emphasized by a message one of the braves carried from Half-King: that the Indians were ready to attack the French, "waiting only for your assistance. . . . If you do not come to our assistance now, we are entirely undone, and I think we shall never meet again."

Washington gathered together his subordinate officers, and they discussed the situation. Despite the odds, the decision was to go forward. At the very least, they had to make a show of force, hoping for the best. As the men renewed their road-work, Washington proceeded to write a flurry of letters to Governor Dinwiddie and, on his own initiative, to the royal governors of Maryland and Pennsylvania, informing them of the situation and requesting troops. He also replied to Half-King using the stylistic flourishes of the day stating that "our hearts burn with love and affection" for Virginia's Indian allies, and that he was happy to state that "a great number of our warriors" and "great guns" were on their way "to assist you."

The French, meanwhile, had not been idle. While Washington's force did its strenuous trail-blazing work, the French added significantly to the fortifications of their settlement. In addition, the troops had been reinforced with an additional 800 men.

After a further delay caused by the spring flood of the Youghiogheny River that made it temporarily impassible, Washington and his men set up a base camp in a field called the Great Meadows. There he took advantage of two depressions in the meadow to construct a rudimentary fort, which he named Fort Necessity. The following day, a frontiersman by the name of Christopher Gist who lived in the area arrived and stated that a party of about 50 Frenchmen had passed near his house the previous day and were still in the area. Washington immediately dispatched scouting parties to discover the exact location of the Frenchmen. While Washington waited for the scouting parties' report, a messenger from Half-King arrived that evening. He informed Washington that Half-King and his braves were camped just six miles away from Washington's position and that he knew the location of the French force. Though the scouts had not yet returned, Washington was anxious to meet with Half-King and attack the French as quickly as possible. Leaving behind part of his group at the fort, Washington took 40 men with him and rendezvoused with Half-King the following day. There the two

This lithograph, printed around 1853, shows George Washington (right, in a dark suit) in the fields at his Mount Vernon, Virginia, estate. Like other plantation owners of the period, Washington owned slaves. (Library of Congress)

A preserved building of Fort Pitt, the name the British gave Fort Duquesne after they captured it from the French. (US Army)

MUSKET: A long-barreled, smooth-bore firearm commonly used by the military from colonial times to the Civil War. It was accurate to a distance of approximately 50 yards.

discussed their plan of attack. After reaching their decision, Washington and his men, together with Half-King and just over a dozen braves, trekked through the forest to the French camp. The plan was simple but effective. When they were near the camp, Half-King and his braves would quietly take up position behind the camp. Washington would divide his force in two and position them on the right and left sides of the camp. Once surrounded, all the attackers would simultaneously fire at the Frenchmen.

Washington was leading the force on the right into position when the French discovered him. With the alarm raised, Washington promptly ordered his men to fire. Quickly after that Washington heard echoing fire from behind the French camp, signifying that Half-King and his braves had reached their position in time for the attack. Even though the two groups were about equally matched in numbers, the French were in a desperate situation and fought hard to defend themselves. Thick clouds of musket smoke from the heavy firing hung in the air. After about 15 minutes of fighting and with their casualties mounting, a group of surviving Frenchmen was caught attempting a breakout, whereupon they threw down their firearms in surrender. As Washington advanced to accept, he was dismayed to see Half-King and his braves fall upon the French in order "to knock the poor, unhappy wounded on the head and bereave them of their scalps." The surviving Frenchmen who could do so dashed toward Washington and his men, pleading for protection. A smaller group of French officers, however, were angrily gesticulating and protesting. One of them pulled from a pouch some official-looking papers and furiously waved them in Washington's face. The chaos around Washington continued for several minutes. When it finally subsided, Washington discovered that he and his men had attacked a force of 32 Frenchmen, killed 10 of them in the battle, and captured the rest. What he also discovered is that one of the dead was the French commander, Joseph Coulon, sieur de Jumonville, an ambassador from the King of France. The ambassador was on a mission to reinforce France's claim to the region. Washington returned with his prisoners to Fort Necessity, where he sent a report to

Governor Dinwiddie who forwarded an account of the event to the British government in London.

News of the incident also reached Paris. The response by the French government and people was immediate and forceful. A French poet said, "The assassination of Jumonville is a monument of perfidy that ought to enrage eternity." The French philosopher Voltaire noted, with exaggeration only on the weapons used, "Such was the complications of political interests that a cannon shot fired in America could give the signal that set Europe in a blaze." In Europe, that "blaze" was named the Seven Years War. In North America, it was known as the French and Indian War. When the fighting ended in 1763, a defeated France surrendered to a victorious England its colonies in North America from the Mississippi River to the Appalachian mountains, including New France (Canada). Voltaire soothed the French monarch King Louis XV, distraught over the loss of the North American possessions, with the words, "After all, Sire, what have we lost-a few acres of snow?" But Voltaire was wrong. Thanks to George Washington, England had become the greatest power in North America and Europe.

An engraving based on a portrait of Washington painted by Rembrandt Peal. (Author's Collection)

The ranks of general officers are as follows:	
Brigadier General:	One Star
Major General:	Two Stars
Lieutenant General:	Three Stars
General:	Four Stars
General of the Army:	Five Stars
General of the Armies:	Congress has never stipulated how the rank should be indicated. It is assumed it would be with six stars.

WINFIELD SCOTT *A Lance Corporal almost Starts a War*

Biography in Brief

WINFIELD SCOTT (1786-1866) participated in five wars, the War of 1812, the Seminole War (1835-1841), Aroostock War (1838), the Mexican War (1846-1848), and the American Civil War (1861-1865).

Scott started his military career with the Virginia militia in 1807. He joined the army and was commissioned a captain of light artillery in 1808. When the War of 1812 began, Scott was a lieutenant colonel. His career rose quickly during the conflict, and he became a brigadier general in 1814. In 1841 he was promoted to major general and in 1855 to brevet lieutenant general.

Age and ill health limited Scott's involvement in the American Civil War. His greatest contribution was the Anaconda Plan, a strategic blockade of Confederate ports. He retired on November 1, 1861, and died at West Point, New York, in 1866. Scott was a general for 47 years, making him America's longest-serving general.

The following account is of the incident that launched his career when he was a lance corporal in the Virginia militia.

The year 1807 was not a good one for the 18-year-old republic, the United States of America. Europe was in the middle of the Napoleonic War, pitting France under Emperor Napoleon I against Great Britain and its allies. The United States had proclaimed itself a neutral nation; thus, in theory, it had the right to do trade with both sides. Great Britain, as part of its effort to defeat France, didn't want the United States to do any business with its enemy. Britain refused to honor its former colony's rights, also known as sovereignty. As an excuse to stop American trade with France, a claim that British sailors were deserting their ships and illegally signing on to be members of American ships' crews. Britain asserted the right of impressment that allowed British men-o'-war (as warships were then called) to stop and board any American ship it encountered and seize sailors claimed to be deserters.

The young republic needed a strong navy to enforce its rights as a nation, but the U.S. Navy at that time was very weak. Great Britain, on the other hand, had the largest and most powerful navy in the world. The British government ordered its fleets to be stationed off the shore of a number of American ports. Many times, in full view of people on shore, a British man-o'-war would intercept an American merchant ship just after it left port. The people on shore would then see the ship boarded and sailors taken away. The U. S. government protested to the British government, but because the U.S. Navy was so weak, the British government ignored the protests.

Things continued this way for two years. Then in 1807, one incident threatened to start a war between the United States and Great Britain. A British fleet had blocked the mouth of Chesapeake Bay. On June 22, 1807, the U.S. Navy frigate, *Chesapeake*, was intercepted just off the coast of Virginia by the larger and more powerful British man-o'-war, HMS *Leopard*. The British captain demanded that a search party be allowed to board the *Chesapeake* in order to seize deserters he claimed were aboard the American vessel. The captain of the *Chesapeake* refused, whereupon the *Leopard* opened fire with its cannon. Caught unprepared, the *Chesapeake* very quickly suffered damage so severe that its captain was forced to surrender in order to save his ship. A British search crew then boarded the helpless *Chesapeake* and took away four crewmen. It was later revealed that one of them, Jenkin Ratford, was a deserter.

News of the attack on the *Chesapeake* outraged the citizens of the United States. Knowing that the country was too weak militarily to go to war against Great Britain, President Thomas Jefferson sought to quiet the calls for war. On July 2, 1807, he issued a proclamation formally barring British men-o'-war from American territorial waters. The proclamation concluded by prohibiting "all supplies and aid" being given to British officers and crew. At that time, it was common for British foraging parties to land on American shores and purchase food, water, and other supplies. The British ignored the ban and continued to send landing parties to obtain supplies.

The most common military force on land in America during this period was the state militia, citizen soldiers who volunteered for military duty whenever the governor declared a crisis that required military intervention. President Jefferson asked Virginia Governor William H. Cabell to activate the state militia and order it to patrol the Virginia coast and stop the British landing parties. One member of the Virginia militia was more than happy to take up arms in the defense of his nation. That man was Lance Corporal Winfield Scott. Standing over six feet tall and strikingly handsome, the 21-year-old Scott literally towered over most men. In civilian life he was a lawyer. When he heard the news of the *Chesapeake* incident, he enthusiastically volunteered. Though he had no formal military training—he had to borrow the uniform he wore—his leadership abilities quickly won him the respect of his superiors. He was promoted to the rank of lance corporal, given command of a squad of cavalry, and ordered to patrol a small inlet near Lynnhaven Bay. From their position Scott and his men were able to clearly see the blockade of British men-o'-war floating in the bay.

One evening Scott received word that a British foraging party had landed upstream of his position, taken on supplies and water, and was on its way back to its ship. Scott promptly ordered his men to take up position along the shore and prepare for an

Lieutenant General Winfield Scott
(Library of Congress)

13

This sketch by F. S. Cozzens depicts the attack by the HMS Leopard *on the USS* Chesapeake *in June 1807, the event that almost caused the War of 1812 to begin in 1807.* (U.S. Naval Historical Center)

DESERTER: In the military, a person who abandons his service without authorization.

ambush. Presently they heard the sound of oars, and soon thereafter, they saw in the gloom the British boat nearing. When the craft, which was hugging the shore, was opposite the position of Scott and his men, Corporal Scott shouted a challenge, "What boat is that?"

"It's His Majesty's Ship *Leopard,* and what the devil is that to you? Give way, my lads!" was the reply.

"I call on you to surrender, sir!" Scott answered and led a mounted charge into the water. The boat was quickly surrounded and the sailors found themselves staring at the leveled muskets and rifles of the militiamen. Because they were unarmed, the foraging crew of eight immediately surrendered and was taken ashore.

Corporal Scott proudly escorted his prisoners back to the militia camp. Since he had not received prior instruction on what to do with any British sailors that he might capture, he decided to keep them in his custody while awaiting further orders. During that time he was more a host than a jailer, showing lavish hospitality to his prisoners.

Meanwhile, Governor Cabell wrote to President Jefferson, requesting instructions. Jefferson, anxious to prevent a war,

A photograph of West Point cadets on parade wearing uniforms in the style used by the army during the War of 1812. (U.S. Army)

ordered that the men be allowed to return to their ship. Scott was angered when he received his orders. He had no argument about letting the crew go. What made him mad was that the praise for his action was tempered by a warning, which he summarized as "Take care not to do it again!"

With the crisis temporarily over, Governor Cabell soon disbanded the militia, Scott returned to his law office, and war fever soon subsided. The taste of military life had been a satisfying one for Scott. With the outbreak of the War of 1812 five years later, he would once again don a uniform, this time in the regular army where he would enter at the rank of captain. Two years after that, in March 1814, at the age of twenty-seven, he would be promoted to the rank of brigadier general.

HMS stands for His Majesty's Ship or Her Majesty's Ship, depending on whether a king or queen is sitting on the British throne. USS stands for United States Ship.

IF YOU'D LIKE TO DISCOVER MORE

The early years of our nation are among the most exciting in our history. Our country was young, largely unexplored, and individual accomplishments seemed limitless. Your local library has many fine books on the period. Here are just a few suggestions:

Fight for Freedom by Benson Bobrick
Liberty! by Thomas Fleming
A History of Us Book 2: Making Thirteen Colonies by Joy Hakim
A History of Us Book 3: From Colonies to Country by Joy Hakim
A History of Us Book 4: The New Nation by Joy Hakim
Struggle for a Continent: The French and Indian Wars by Betsy Maestro
The War of 1812 by Andrew Santella
George Washington Our First Leader by Augusta Stevenson

Chapter

2

A YOUNG NATION'S CHALLENGES

1846~1865

 **MEXICAN WAR**

The Mexican War was the result of two conflicting forces that came to a head in 1846. The first was the belief in the United States of "Manifest Destiny," a phrase used by U.S. political leaders and journalists to explain and justify westward expansion of the United States. John L. O'Sullivan was the first to put into words the belief that citizens of the young United States had in themselves and the future of their nation. His article for *The United States Democratic Review* in November 1839, said in part, "The far-reaching, the boundless future will be the era of American greatness. . . . [T]he nation of many nations is destined to manifest to mankind the excellence of divine principles." The second force was that of Mexican independence. Mexico had won its war for independence from Spain in 1821, but economic and political instability kept the country weak, and recovery was slow and difficult.

Mexicans were also suspicious of the United States. When the U.S. government attempted to purchase the northern Mexican territories of New Mexico and California and when the Mexican territory of Texas, populated by many people from the United States, declared and won its independence from Mexico in 1836, many Mexicans believed it was all part of a sinister plot to cheat and rob Mexico of its northern territories. These suspicions seemed confirmed when the republic of Texas joined the United States in 1845. Relations between the two nations rapidly deteriorated. In early 1846, a military action in the disputed territory between the Nueces and Rio Grande Rivers caused President James K. Polk to ask Congress to declare war, which it did on May 13, 1846.

Winfield Scott was the United States' senior general. The initial fighting was along the Mexico/Texas border and led by general Zachary Taylor against the Mexican dictator, General Santa Anna. Taylor would remain in the north while Scott launched an offensive that began with a landing at the Mexican port of Veracruz. His army's series of victories over Santa Anna and his armies, combined with the capture of Mexico City, and the exile of Santa Anna brought a close to the war. When the war officially ended with the Treaty of Guadalupe Hidalgo in February 1848, the United States obtained the Mexican territories it had wanted, paying Mexico an indemnity of $15 million.

Many of the generals who achieved greatness in the American Civil War, including Robert E. Lee, Ulysses S. Grant, and Thomas J. Jackson, were junior officers who learned the hard art of war and earned glory in the plains and mountains of Mexico during the Mexican War.

 ## THE AMERICAN CIVIL WAR

The American Civil War, also known as the War of the Rebellion and the War Between the States, was the largest and most terrible conflict on United States soil. The root cause of the war was slavery. The growing crisis between the non-slave-holding states of the North and the slave states of the South finally reached the breaking point with the election of Abraham Lincoln as president in 1860. Southern slave-holding states feared that the new president would try to both prevent the spread of slavery to new states in the West, and eliminate it in states where it already existed. Seven southern states, South Carolina, Mississippi, Florida, Alabama, Georgia, Louisiana, and Texas, seceded from the United States soon after Lincoln's election and announced the formation of the Confederate States of America.

The first battle in the American Civil War occurred in April 1861, when the Confederates attacked and seized the Union Fort Sumter that guarded Charleston harbor. Within a few weeks the secessionist states were joined by four more, Virginia, Arkansas, North Carolina, and Tennessee. From the beginning, Lincoln was determined to keep the Union intact, and called for volunteers to suppress the rebellion. Congress supported this view as well, and voted almost unanimously for a resolution presented by Senator John J. Crittenden of Kentucky shortly after the Union defeat at First Manassas, also called the First Battle of Bull Run, in 1861. It declared

". . . that this war is not waged . . . for any purpose of conquest or subjugation, nor purpose of overthrowing . . . established institutions . . . but to defend . . . the Constitution and to preserve the Union."

For the South, Jefferson Davis, President of the Confederate States of America, stated in 1863 that the secessionists were "forced to take up arms to vindicate the political rights, the freedom, equality, and State sovereignty which were the heritage purchased by the blood of our revolutionary sires."

Both sides believed it would be a short, relatively bloodless war. They thought that after a couple of sharp engagements, the defeated side would recognize the rightness of the victor's cause and capitulate. The Union did not surrender after First Manassas, however, and in the spring of 1862 at the Battle of Shiloh, both sides received a bloody foretaste of the total war to come. Three more years of terrible fighting would pass. Two percent of the population, approximately 620,000 men, would perish before an end was finally reached.

On May 10, 1865, President Andrew Johnson declared that the Civil War was over. The Union had won. Though healing the scars left by the conflict would take generations, the United States of America had survived its greatest challenge.

ROBERT E. LEE *Saved by a Fallen Tree*

The Mexican dictator, General Santa Anna liked to call himself the "Napoleon of the West." Although he was skilled in the military arts, he was not the equal of Napoleon I, the man who in the opening years of the 1800s, had been the master of all of Europe. Santa Anna's efforts to keep Texas a Mexican territory reached their zenith with his victory at the Alamo in 1836 and ended with his crushing defeat weeks later at San Jacinto. Shortly thereafter, he was forced into exile. When hostilities appeared imminent between the United States and Mexico, Santa Anna successfully returned to power and was determined to not only defeat the United States armies but also regain territory that had been lost.

Unfortunately for his country, his military ambition was greater than his military skills. After his army was defeated at Buena Vista in Northern Mexico by General Zachary Taylor and his army, the Americans thought Santa Anna's rule was over, but he surprised them. Instead of surrendering, Santa Anna retreated south to Mexico City. Then in the mountains between Mexico City and the gulf port of Veracruz, Santa Anna reorganized his army and began constructing strong fortifications in order to block any attempt to advance onto Mexico City. Everyone on both sides realized that if the capital of Mexico fell, the war would be over. One of the strongest fortifications was near the mountain of Serra Gordo, which overlooked the only road the advancing American army under General Winfield Scott could use in its march to Mexico City.

General Scott and his army were encamped at the foothills of the mountains on the Rio del Plan. Time was working against General Scott. Yellow fever season—called the *vomito*—was approaching, and if his army stayed where it was, the disease would decimate it. Also, Scott had to worry about the men in his ranks whose enlistments were due to expire soon. If he didn't move fast enough, he would literally find himself a general without an army. Finally, Scott's supply situation was precarious. Everything had to be transported by sailing ship from the United States and then overland by horse- or ox-drawn wagons. Just the transport from ports in the United States to Veracruz took weeks. In addi-

Biography in Brief
ROBERT EDWARD LEE (1807-1870) was one of America's greatest generals, though he was never a general in the U.S. Army. Lee graduated from West Point. He fought in the Mexican War (1846-1848) and the American Civil War (1861-1865). He served as superintendent at West Point (1852-1855). When his home state of Virginia seceded in 1861, Lee resigned his commission as a colonel in the Union army. He was commissioned a brigadier general in the Confederate army and military advisor to Jefferson Davis, president of the Confederacy. On June 1, 1862, he was appointed commanding general of the Army of Northern Virginia, and on August 31, 1861, he was promoted to general.

In 1864, Lee found himself fighting General Ulysses Grant, who served with Lee under General Scott in the Mexican War. Lee surrendered to Grant at Appomattox on April 9, 1865. After the war Lee became the president of Washington University where he died in 1870. After his death the university changed its name to Washington and Lee University.

The following account occurred during the Mexican War at a crucial period in General Scott's campaign in which Lee's initiative in the rugged terrain of the Pedregal would prove decisive.

ENLISTMENT: In the military, the period of time an individual serves in the armed forces.

Robert E. Lee in a photograph taken by Matthew Brady shortly after the Civil War. (Library of Congress)

tion supply caravans under armed escort had to run the dangerous gauntlet of bandits and bands of Mexican soldiers who openly roamed the road between Veracruz and Scott's army.

Scott had solved part of his supply problem by having his army live off the land, a policy that could only be maintained if his army kept advancing; otherwise, his men and pack animals would soon consume all the food and forage in the immediate area and starve to death. The two-part question for General Scott was: which sec-

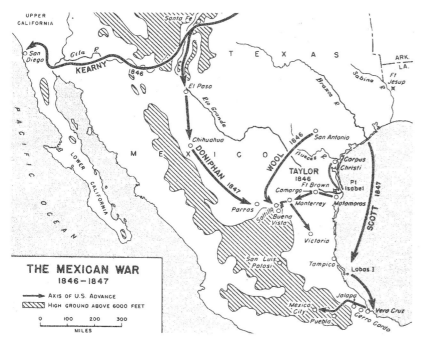

THE MEXICAN WAR
1846–1847

→ AXIS OF U.S. ADVANCE
///// HIGH GROUND ABOVE 6000 FEET

0   100   200   300
MILES

A map of the campaigns against Mexico, including General Phil Kearny's campaign in California, General Alexander Doniphan and General Zachary Taylor's campaign in the north, and General Winfield Scott's campaign from Veracruz to Mexico City.
(U.S. Army)

tion of the Mexican defenses was vulnerable and could it be found in time for the American army to exploit it? The army's only hope lay in finding a way through the rugged ravines of the Pedregal along the Mexican left flank.

Robert E. Lee was a handsome captain of engineers in Scott's army. Tall, calm, and intelligent, he had graduated second in his class in 1929 at West Point. He had already gained recognition for his engineering work on the Mississippi River near St. Louis and the New York harbor defenses. Now he faced the most daunting challenge of his young career. As he later wrote, "The right of the Mexican line rested on the river at a perpendicular rock, unscalable by man or beast, and their left on impassable ravines; the main road was defended by field works containing thirty-five cannon; in their rear was the mountain of Cerro Gordo, surrounded by entrenchments in which were cannon and crowned by a tower overlooking all—it was around this army that it was intended to lead our troops." Somehow he would have to find a route that could be constructed into a road capable of bearing Scott's army.

On the morning of April 15, 1847, Lee and his guide, John Fitzwalter, set out on a reconnaissance mission to discover a path around the Mexican army. The two men managed to penetrate the Mexican lines without being discovered. As they explored, mark-

Lieutenant Robert E. Lee.
(U.S. Army)

21

A lithograph showing the U.S. Army siege of Veracruz. Lee supervised the construction of the artillery positions. General Scott used cannon from the navy warships to breach the walls of the city. (U.S. Army)

BLAZE: A mark or other indication, usually on a tree, used to signify the location of a trail.

ing their trail and keeping alert for any approaching enemy, Lee's experienced eye readily saw that Santa Anna had chosen his defensive locations well. One ridge after another contained formidable defenses of cannon and infantry. Slowly and carefully, Lee and Fitzwalter continued their reconnaissance along the Mexican army's left flank. Lee soon discovered what he thought was a vulnerable spot that was undefended. As he suspected, a road would have to be constructed along the trail he had blazed. It wouldn't be easy, but he saw that it was possible. The two men continued their searching, and eventually they came upon a spring and a well-trodden path to it from the south. Lee expanded his search around the immediate area and decided that he had successfully reached the rear of the Mexican army's left flank. Now it was time to return and give the good news to General Scott.

Just as they were getting ready to head back, however, they heard the sound of Mexican soldiers approaching. Retreat down the route they had taken was impossible. It was too exposed. They'd be seen before they had traveled far. Their only chance of avoiding capture was to hide among the brush and logs that bordered the spring. Quickly, Lee slid under a large log that lay close to the spring, burrowing behind the thick undergrowth along its side. Fitzwalter meanwhile managed to find a hiding spot in nearby brush. Within moments, a group of unsuspecting Mexican soldiers casually approached what was the local watering hole for the troops in the area. They drank the water and rested in the shade of the trees. Captain Lee scarcely allowed himself to breathe.

An illustration showing the uniforms soldiers in General Scott's army wore at the time of the Mexican War. (U.S. Army)

Evidence of their presence was obvious in the soft banks of the spring where Lee and Fitzwalter's distinctive and fresh boot prints marked the earth. If one Mexican soldier looked down and decided to question the tracks, Lee knew a search would begin and they'd be captured.

More soldiers arrived, replacing the men of the first group who returned to their posts. One man in this second group approached the log hiding Lee and sat on it. Another soldier joined him. They were only three feet away from Lee who dared not move a muscle even though he was soaked to the skin and had insects crawling into his clothing and biting him. Eventually they got up and left. Even so, Lee still could not relax. Other soldiers arrived. One even stepped over the log and almost on Lee.

Hours passed. One group of Mexican soldiers after another

A detail from a Currier & Ives illustration of General Scott's landing at Veracruz.
(U.S. Army)

came and went, yet amazingly, none of them discovered Lee and Fitzwalter. Eventually, with the sun beginning to set, fewer groups of Mexican soldiers came to the spring. When darkness fell, they finally stopped. Only after he felt sure that there would be no more soldiers coming did the cold, stiff, and tired Lee slowly emerge from underneath his sanctuary and reunite with an equally exhausted Fitzwalter. Although they were out of immediate danger, they were far from safe. Not only were they still deep behind enemy lines, it was now night and they had to retrace their steps over treacherous terrain in near total darkness.

Fortunately, when he was a boy, Lee had spent many days and nights exploring the countryside near his home in Virginia. As a result, he had developed a sure foot and a keen sense of direction. Hours later, the two successfully reached American lines. With a filthy uniform testifying to his ordeal, an exhausted Lee reported his good news of a path.

General Scott ordered further reconnaissance, which confirmed Lee's report. Events proceeded quickly and on April 17, two days after Lee's discovery, General Scott's army defeated Santa Anna's troops in the Battle of Cerro Gordo. It was a three-hour fight that routed the Mexican army and allowed Scott's army to begin its advance to Mexico City.

Instead of awarding medals to soldiers for outstanding service, senior officers would honor good performance by writing about it in their official reports and by giving the soldiers a brevet promotion. Brevets, while raising the officer's rank, did not increase his pay or authority. Robert E. Lee was breveted a major for his service at Cerro Gordo. At the later battles of Contreras and Churubusco, he was breveted a lieutenant colonel. He received a third brevet, to colonel, at the battle of Chapultepec.

ULYSSES S. GRANT *The Reluctant Priest at San Cosme*

Biography in Brief

ULYSSES S. GRANT (1822-1885) was born Hiram Ulysses Grant. He fought in the Mexican War (1846-1848) and the American Civil War (1861-1865). He changed his name when, upon his arrival at West Point in 1839, he discovered that a clerical error had him registered as Ulysses Simpson Grant. He graduated from West Point in 1843. During the Mexican War he served with distinction. He resigned from the army in 1854.

When the American Civil War broke out, he returned to the military as a colonel of volunteers in 1861. He was promoted to brigadier general in 1861. Grant's successes in the Western Theater saw him rise in rank, command, and responsibility. On March 12, 1864, Lieutenant General Grant was made General in Chief of the Armies of the United States. In this role he defeated the Confederate armies in 1865.

In 1868, he was elected to the first of two terms as President of the United States. Years later, dying of throat cancer and bankrupt because of a series of bad financial investments, Grant began writing his memoirs in order to provide for his family. He finished the manuscript only four days before his death on July 23, 1885.

The following account occurred during the Mexican War. Grant saw an opportunity to turn the tide of battle and seized it.

Lieutenant Ulysses S. Grant began the Mexican War as a regimental quartermaster. Few jobs in the military, then and now, are more demanding and less glamorous. A quartermaster must make sure that soldiers have everything they need for food, shelter, clothing, supplies, and transportation. The duty is even more demanding when the army is on the march through hostile territory. Grant's challenges during the Mexican War were particularly daunting. With lines of communication and supply long, primitive, and subject to breakdown through ambush, weather, or incompetence, it was not unknown for an army to become dependent on its own resources, that is, living off the land as best it could until supplies arrived. Important as the role of quartermaster was, Grant hated the position and tried to get out of it. Years later, Grant, who rarely swore, said he would ". . . excuse those who may have done so, if they were in charge of a train of Mexican pack mules at the time."

As General Scott's army marched toward Mexico City from Veracruz, Grant successfully contracted with local Mexicans to supply shoes, clothing, and bread. He also led foraging missions to purchase horses, mules, and livestock that because of loss, sickness, or injury, constantly needed replacement.

It was at the town of San Cosme that Grant would get the opportunity to drop his quartermaster duties and lead men in battle. Troops led by General William Worth had run up against a determined Mexican defense entrenched behind tall, thick fortifications. Grant, observing the unfolding attack, saw what he thought was a way to dislodge the defenders. Off to one side of the battle was a church with a tall bell tower. Grant believed that if he could get a small cannon up to the top of the bell tower, he could "outflank" the defenses by firing down into the Mexican lines.

Quickly Grant made his proposal to his commanding officer, Colonel Garland, and received permission to begin putting words into action. Getting to the church would be no easy task.

Lieutenant Ulysses Grant at the time of the Mexican War. (U.S. Army)

One of the lightest cannon in the U.S. Army during this period was the 12-pounder mountain howitzer. At that time cannon were classified by the weight of their shell; thus, this cannon fired a projectile weighing 12 pounds. The 12-pounder was small (its gun tube was less than three feet long), and it was designed for easy transport and assembly. Even so, the gun tube that fired the projectile weighed 220 pounds, the carriage (which held the tube and if necessary could be disassembled) weighed 157 pounds when assembled, and the wheels, which were 38 inches in diameter, weighed 65 pounds each. Ammunition boxes, which carried eight rounds, weighed 112 pounds. Added to this were the accessories necessary to clear and fire the cannon including the sponge and rammer staff, the lanyard, and a long pole with a double-screw twist of metal at the end called a "worm."

Grant and his men would have to hand-carry, or drag (accounts are not specific here) everything to the church. Since there was a battle raging, this group (again, Grant doesn't say how many men) could hardly take the easiest and most direct

BELFRY: The part of a tower or steeple where bells are hung.

Mexican dictator Santa Anna fleeing Cerro Gordo. (Author's Collection)

route. Once everything had been distributed, Grant led his men on a detour through several ditches, some which had water up to their chests!

The force made it to the church without suffering any casualties from enemy fire, but the adventure was not yet over for the group. Grant began pounding on the locked door to summon the priest. "A priest came to the door, who, while extremely polite, declined to admit us," Grant later recalled. At that point, Grant could very easily have ordered his men to smash down the door, overpower the priest, and barge into the church. Instead, he chose the path of summary diplomacy. As he explained in his autobiography, *The Personal Memoirs of Ulysses S. Grant,* "With the little Spanish then at my command, I explained to him that he might save property by opening the door, and he certainly would save himself from becoming a prisoner, for a time at least; and besides, I intended to go in whether he consented or not. He began to see his duty in the same light that I did, and opened the door, though he did not look as if it gave him special pleasure to do so."

His summary diplomacy successful, Grant and his men climbed up to the belfry, assembled the cannon, and began firing down into the Mexican defenders. A prompt, new attack by General Worth's troops successfully breached the defenses and the Mexican army was routed. General Worth was so pleased by Grant's actions that he singled out Grant for praise in dispatches to the government, a great honor in those days.

> **Ulysses Grant was such a poor student in school that fellow students gave him the nickname "Useless Grant."**

Lieutenant General Grant in 1864 at Cold Harbor, Virginia. (Library of Congress)

THOMAS JACKSON *A Dramatic Stand at Chapultepec*

Biography in Brief

THOMAS JONATHAN "STONE-WALL" JACKSON (1824-1863) fought in the Mexican War(1846-1848) and the American Civil War (1861-1865). Like Robert E. Lee, under whom he served in the Army of Northern Virginia, Jackson became a general in the Confederate army, not the Union army.

Jackson graduated from West Point in 1846 and served with distinction in the Mexican War where he was breveted a major. In 1852 he resigned and became an instructor at Virginia Military Institute. When Virginia joined the Confederacy, Jackson joined the Confederate army and was appointed a brigadier general on June 17, 1861, promoted to major general on October 7, 1861, and to lieutenant general on October 10, 1862. During the Battle of Chancellorsville on May 2, 1863, he was accidentally shot and wounded in the left arm by friendly fire. His left arm was amputated. During his convalescence he contracted pneumonia and died on May 10, 1863.

The following account is of Jackson's stand against the Mexican army at a critical point in the fight for Chapultepec, the final barrier protecting Mexico City.

The castle of Chapultepec was located on the summit of a 200-foot-high hill that commanded the southern approaches to Mexico City. If General Scott and his army could take Chapultepec, the way to Mexico City would be wide open and victory in the Mexican War would be assured. The castle was large and imposing. As it housed Mexico's military college and was a strategically important defense, Scott was certain the castle would be well defended.

First Lieutenant Thomas Jackson was in command of a section of artillery composed of two horse-drawn, six-pounder cannon. His company commander was Captain John B. Magruder, a handsome, vain, and dramatic officer whose love of pageantry had earned him the nickname "Prince John." Magruder's company was in Major General Gideon Pillow's division, one of four in Lieutenant General Scott's army. Pillow's division, together with a division led by Major General John Quitman, was ordered to attack the southern and western walls of the castle. The attack itself would be made by infantry led by Colonel William Trousdale. In support of the attack, Magruder's company was stationed on the far left flank and under orders to stop any reinforcements coming from Mexico City and block any attempt at escape by the defenders in the castle. General Pillow had given Jackson specific orders enabling him to act independently of Magruder if it became necessary in the heat of the battle.

On the morning of September 13, 1847, after an artillery barrage that lasted just over two hours, Colonel Trousdale led the attack on Chapultepec. The infantry had covered just over 1,300 yards when it came under heavy defensive cannon and small arms fire. Trousdale went down, wounded. The fire from the Mexican positions was so heavy and accurate that the infantry could neither advance nor retreat. Realizing that the infantry would be annihilated unless something drastic was done to turn the tide, Jackson ordered his two guns to advance. In a letter he later wrote to his sister, Laura, he stated that they took up position ". . . in a road which was swept

Lieutenant General Thomas Jonathan Jackson, CSA. (National Archives)

with grape[shot] and canister, and at the same time thousands of muskets from the castle itself pouring down like hail." Before Jackson and his men could unlimber the cannon from the horses, he later recounted that a battery of Mexican artillery ". . . opened fire, and at the first discharge, killed or disabled every one of the twelve horses of my two guns."

The situation quickly worsened. One of the cannon was damaged and useless because it could not be freed from the dead horses hitched to it. Under continued fire from the castle, Jackson's now demoralized men ducked for cover behind

When Jackson attended West Point, one of the regulations was that cadets had to bathe once a week. If a cadet wished to do so more often, he had to request permission from the superintendent.

29

John B. Magruder. A captain in the Union army at the time of the Mexican War, like Jackson, he became a Confederate general in the Civil War. (United States Army Military History Institute)

any rock or bush they could find. Though his men were near panic, Jackson refused to give into fear. Striding along the road, with bullets kicking up dust and glancing off boulders all around him, Jackson attempted to rally his men. "There is no danger!" he shouted. "See? I am not hit!" But his men refused to budge from their refuges. Suddenly, a Mexican cannon ball flew in between Jackson's widespread legs. One sergeant then stood up and helped Jackson return fire with their one usable cannon. A private then crawled forward to help, but Jackson ordered him to head back to the rear and get reinforcements.

Meanwhile, Major General William Worth, commander of one of the divisions assigned to reinforce the attack, had ridden forward to observe the progress of the attack. He witnessed Jackson's lone stand and sent him orders to cease fire and retreat. Jackson refused. Even though they were in an exposed position within point-blank range of the enemy cannon, Jackson sent back the message that it was more dangerous to fall back than it was to stay where they were and fight it out with the enemy. While General Worth was calling up reinforcements, Captain Magruder, braving the heavy fire, galloped toward Jackson's position. Just before he reached it, his horse was shot out from under him. Despite this, Magruder was unharmed. He picked himself up and, together with a couple of Jackson's men, managed to free, repair, and position the second cannon.

His battery was now at full strength: two small cannon against multiple batteries and other forces. Despite the odds against him, Jackson traded two-shot volley after two-shot volley with the heavy salvoes and musket fire of the Mexican artillery and infantry. Somehow Jackson held his own until a brigade sent by General Worth arrived, stormed the castle, and breached the walls. Soon thereafter Chapultepec was captured. Anxious to press on before General Santa Anna could rally defenses in Mexico City, General Scott wanted to continue as soon as he had restored order to his ranks. Jackson, by this time, had found fresh horses and limbers for his cannon. When he heard the orders to advance, he quickly led his section up the path of attack along one of the causeways. Jackson soon came upon about 40 infantrymen commanded by

The Battle of Chapultepec. (U.S. Army)

Lieutenants Harvey Hill and Barnard E. Bee. The three officers discovered that they had moved so quickly that they had exceeded their orders and were now a mile in advance of the main body of Scott's army. The three discussed what to do next. Jackson offered to provide artillery support if Hill and Bee decided to continue. Just then Captain Magruder, on a new horse, found them and ordered everyone to fall back. The three immediately begged the captain to allow them to continue up the causeway. Magruder was someone who could easily be convinced that an attack was always better than a retreat. As a result, he agreed to let them go forward.

The small combined force advanced an additional half-mile when suddenly it came upon a Mexican cavalry unit composed of about 1,500 lancers. Despite being outnumbered approximately 20 to 1, Jackson quickly deployed his two cannon in preparation for action. As he later reported, "I opened up on [the lancers] and [with] every fire we cut lanes through them." As the Mexicans fell back, the Americans advanced. Jackson recalled, "[We] pursued at full gallop until the bullets of their rear guns began to fall near the leaders, then we would

LIMBER: A two-wheeled, horse-drawn vehicle that carries ammunition and powder behind which a cannon is towed.

General Winfield Scott and his army enter Mexico City. (U.S. Army)

When Jackson was accepted as a cadet at West Point, he was one of six orphans in his class. Twenty-two others in his graduating class of fifty-nine had only one living parent.

unlimber [the cannon] and pour it into them-then limber up and pursue. We kept it up for about a mile."

With other elements of Scott's force closing in on the city, the fight for Mexico City ended that night. In the darkness, General Santa Anna slipped away and, for the final time, went into exile. Soon thereafter, Mexico would formally surrender by signing the Treaty of Guadalupe Hidalgo.

Lieutenant Jackson, meanwhile, was a hero. Captain Magruder in a dispatch wrote, in part, "If devotion, industry, talent and gallantry are the highest qualities of a soldier, then [Lieutenant Jackson] is entitled to the distinction which their possession confers." General Scott also praised Jackson in his dispatch to the president and Congress. Jackson would receive two brevets, rising to the rank of major.

GEORGE CUSTER *And the Triumph of the Union Cavalry at Brandy Station*

Biography in Brief

GEORGE ARMSTRONG CUSTER (1839–1876) fought in the American Civil War (1861–1865) and in the Indian Wars (1867–1890) in the Great Plains. He graduated last in his class of twenty-four at West Point in 1861. He was promoted to captain in June 1862. On June 28, 1863, Custer was promoted to brigadier general of volunteers. In September 1864, he was breveted major general of volunteers. In the postwar reduction and reorganization of the Army, Custer reverted to his permanent rank of captain in the regular army. In 1866, he was promoted to lieutenant colonel.

Custer participated in a number of campaigns against the Plains Indians. On June 25, 1876, while leading the 7th Cavalry, Custer attacked a combined Sioux and Cheyenne camp near the Little Big Horn River in Montana Territory. He and his immediate command were massacred. It is ironic that Custer is remembered for his defeat at Little Big Horn and not for his heroism and victories during the Civil War where he was considered among the Union's greatest cavalry leaders.

This account is of his participation in the Battle of Brandy Station during the Civil War.

The Civil War was in its third year when Captain George Armstrong Custer returned to the Union's Army of the Potomac on April 16, 1863, following a two-month furlough. As soon as he arrived at camp, he was ordered to present himself to his new commanding officer, Brigadier General Alfred Pleasonton. As soon as Pleasonton saw the handsome, 23-year-old captain, he came straight to the point. "Curly," he said, using the nickname inspired by Custer's long, curly hair, "I want you as my special aide. I'll make no bones about it: you're a man after my own heart. Pure rambunction. Well, will you accept?"

Custer enthusiastically shook the general's hand as he agreed. Custer had not seen action since the Battle of First Manassas, or Bull Run, two years earlier, and from the very beginning, he had attracted attention for his dash and daring, which was why Pleasonton, a general of cavalry in the Army of the Potomac, was so anxious to have him. Up to that time, the Army of the Potomac's cavalry had been beaten to the point of humiliation by the Confederate cavalry led by General J.E.B. "Jeb" Stuart. Pleasonton was determined to reverse the Union cavalry's poor reputation, and he was counting on men like Custer to help him achieve that goal.

Pleasonton's first real opportunity came at the Battle of Chancellorsville on May 3, 1863. Although General Joseph Hooker's Army of the Potomac suffered another humbling defeat at the hand of General Robert E. Lee's Army of Northern Virginia, the one bright spot for the Union was the role played by Pleasonton's cavalry. During the chaos of the Union army's retreat, Pleasonton managed to deploy a blocking force at Hazel Grove that successfully blunted the Confederate counterattack led by Lee's "right arm," General Thomas "Stonewall" Jackson. Pleasonton's cavalry paid a high price for their defense. One unit, the 8th Pennsylvania Cavalry, containing about 500 men, was almost completely wiped out. The important fact was that the Army of the Potomac would live to fight another day. In gratitude, General

Cadet George Armstrong Custer, West Point Class of 1861. (West Point Museum)

BATTERY: A group of cannon.

Hooker appointed Pleasonton his new Commanding Officer of the Cavalry Corps. For the next month, the Army of the Potomac licked its wounds.

Then, on June 6, 1863, with Custer and other subordinates watching, Hooker discussed his army's next move with Pleasonton and his other subordinate generals. Scouts had reported that the Army of Northern Virginia was on the move north. Hooker believed that Lee was planning another invasion of the North. Such a move would leave Richmond, the capital of the Confederacy, exposed to capture. Seizing Richmond had long been a goal of the Union. Hooker saw this as the opportunity to succeed where his predecessor, General George McClellan, had failed. "We've got to stop [Lee] before he crosses the Potomac," Hooker said. "Jeb Stuart is covering his right with ten thousand horse. Knock out Stuart and you paralyze Lee." Hooker told Pleasonton that he had learned that Stuart's men would be camped at a place called Brandy Station. He ordered Pleasonton to attack Stuart there. Hooker believed if Pleasonton acted quickly, the element of surprise would work in his favor. Hooker concluded by saying, "If you can't cut him to pieces, at least shake him up—put him on the run, harass him—anything to stop Lee dead in his tracks."

Pleasonton quickly drew up his plans. He would split his command into two units. One would cross the Rappahannock River at Beverly Ford and strike at Stuart. The second would cross at Kelly's Ford and create a diversion at Culpeper Courthouse where the bulk of Lee's army was encamped.

On June 9, just before dawn, Pleasonton's Cavalry Corps mounted up and rode off to battle. Custer and Pleasonton were in the unit that crossed at Beverly Ford. A thick mist covered the meadow, keeping the Union cavalry hidden as it approached Brandy Station. When scouts reported they were near their objective, Pleasonton ordered his men to rein in and wait. Then Pleasonton and Custer quietly rode ahead to reconnoiter. Using their spyglasses, they discovered a Confederate camp composed of two divisions of cavalry. So far they hadn't been spotted, but Pleasonton knew that they'd have to act fast. Quickly he reached a decision. Pointing to two batteries of horse artillery deployed to defend the camp, Pleasonton

ordered Custer to take the 1st Brigade, 1st Division, and seize the artillery. "Don't stop till they're yours. Understood?" Pleasonton asked. Custer stared at his commanding officer in surprise, then nodded. He was only a captain, and an aide— essentially a glorified messenger. Now he was being given a command normally held by a colonel! Custer realized that Pleasonton was giving him a chance to really prove himself. If he succeeded, he would be promoted.

Pleasonton quickly laid out the rest of his plan. While Custer and his men attacked the cannon batteries, Pleasonton would lead the main attack on the camp. Pleasonton conclud-ed by saying that once he had the batteries, "Guard 'em with your life."

Pleasonton then rode off to organize his attack. Custer rode to the 1st Brigade and informed its commander, Colonel

George Custer (right), lying on the ground with his dog, enjoying a camp lunch with a group of fellow officers. A lover of animals, Custer always had a dog with him in camp. (Library of Congress)

35

Custer was a class clown at West Point. His practical jokes and pranks almost caused him to be expelled. One time during Spanish class, he asked the professor how to say, "Class dismissed" in Spanish. When the teacher did so, Custer, who held the cadet rank of squad leader, marched the class out of the room.

Major General George Armstrong Custer. (Library of Congress)

Benjamin F. "Grimes" Davis, of Pleasonton's orders. Fortunately, Davis, a hero who had recently been breveted a brigadier general, liked Custer and understood what Pleasonton was doing. Graciously he turned over his command.

Once Custer has his men in position, Custer drew his saber, waved it in the air and shouted, "Charge!" At the same time,

Pleasonton's force galloped out of the mist straight for the camp. Stuart's "Invincibles," as they were known, were taken by surprise. Within minutes the battle became a mad, swirling mass of horses and men, of blue and butternut uniforms.

One Confederate artilleryman fired his pistol point-blank at Custer, the bullet coming so close to Custer's head that it burned his ear. Custer slashed at the man with his saber, felling him. Colonel Davis, who accompanied the attack, was shot dead. At one point, it seemed that the Confederate artillery-men would rout Custer's force. But Custer rallied his command and beat back a determined counterattack.

POINT-BLANK: Aiming and shooting at a target from such close range that a miss is rare.

Meanwhile, General Pleasonton pressed his advantage, driving the disorganized Confederate troops several miles. At Brandy Station, Jeb Stuart succeeded in restoring control and successfully organized a defense. Seeing that further fighting risked turning his victory into a defeat, Pleasonton broke off action.

When he returned to the scene of the original battle, Custer proudly presented his commanding officer with two batteries of Confederate artillery, a large group of prisoners, and a large, gold-trimmed silk Confederate battle flag inscribed, "From the Ladies of Charlottesville to Stuart's Horse Artillery, Our Brave Defenders."

The Battle of Brandy Station was the largest cavalry action of the Civil War. More importantly, as Colonel Charles S. Wainwright later wrote, it improved "the morale of our cavalry, so that they are not now afraid to meet the 'Rebs' on equal terms." Custer was cited for "gallantry throughout the fight." The honors would continue. On June 26, 1863, the Army of the Potomac was camped at Camp Frederick. Night had fallen, and it had been raining for several hours by the time Custer had finished his inspection of the camp's defenses. When he entered the headquarters tent, he was greeted with a chorus of good-natured salutations from his fellow junior officers: "Gentlemen, General Custer!" "Good evening, General!" "How are you, General?" and the like. Custer blushed. He had often boasted that he'd make general in the war, but as he was still a captain after about three years of fighting, that claim now seemed very hollow. Custer vainly tried to hide his

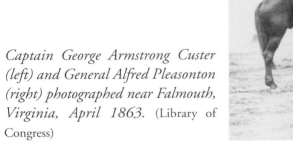

Captain George Armstrong Custer (left) and General Alfred Pleasonton (right) photographed near Falmouth, Virginia, April 1863. (Library of Congress)

embarrassment, which only caused the group to continue. Custer had a fiery temper, and just as it seemed ready to burst out, one of his friends, Lieutenant George W. Yates, pointed to a nearby table. "Look on the table, old fellow. We're not pulling your leg."

Puzzled, Custer walked over and saw a large official envelope. Custer stared at it in shock. Written on the envelope were the words "Brig.-Gen'l. George A. Custer, U.S. Vols." At age 23, Custer had gone from captain to brigadier general and became the youngest general in U.S. Army history.

A sketch by noted Civil War artist Alfred Waud shows a Confederate officer (right) bearing a truce flag approaching Brigadier General George Armstrong Custer (middle left). (Library of Congress)

ARTHUR MacARTHUR *The "Miracle at Missionary Ridge"*

The Union Army of the Cumberland was trapped in Chattanooga, after suffering a humiliating defeat in the Battle of Chickamauga in September 1863. The Confederate Army of Tennessee under General Braxton Bragg had followed up its success by chasing the Union army and taking up position in the high ground around the city. Bragg's army was too weak to attack Chattanooga. One reason was that Bragg, who had a reputation for being irascible, had argued so much with his generals, that there was open rebellion against him within his own ranks. Despite the bickering, after his army had established defensive fortifications, Bragg was still strong enough to keep the Union troops trapped in the city.

Meanwhile the Union army in Chattanooga got a new commander. General Ulysses S. Grant, who had wrestled a 12-pound cannon to the top of a church belfry in Mexico 16 years before. President Abraham Lincoln had made him the new theater commander. General George Thomas, whose nickname was "The Rock of Chickamauga," because of his successful defense during that battle, commanded the army that was trapped inside the city. Another new arrival was William T. Sherman, another famous Union general and a good friend of Grant's. Together they planned to break out of the city and drive off the Confederate army. The plan was to attack the Confederates on both of their flanks. General Joseph Hooker would attack one flank on Lookout Mountain, and Sherman would attack the other flank at a small hill, which, since it was above a railroad tunnel, was called Tunnel Hill. Thomas, meanwhile, would hold his force in reserve in the center.

Eighteen-year-old Captain Arthur MacArthur was the adjutant of the 24th Wisconsin regiment that was part of Thomas's army. He may have been disappointed that he and his unit were not asked to take part in the attacks against the Confederate flanks. Then news arrived that, although Hooker's attack had gone well, Sherman's attack on Tunnel Hill had bogged down. To take pressure off Sherman, Grant ordered Thomas to have his men attack the Rebel center on

Biography in Brief
ARTHUR MacARTHUR (1845-1912) fought in the American Civil War (1861-1865), the Spanish-American War (1898), and the Philippine Insurrection (1899-1903). He was appointed first lieutenant in the 24th Wisconsin Infantry on August 4, 1862, breveted captain for gallantry at the Battle of Perryville in October 1862, promoted to major in January 1864, breveted lieutenant colonel on March 1865, and three months later breveted colonel.

Following the end of the Civil War, he briefly left military service. In February 1866, he enlisted in the regular army as a second lieutenant, five months later he was promoted to captain. Upon the outbreak of the Spanish-American War, he was appointed brigadier general of volunteers in May 1889. In the fall of 1889, he was promoted to major general of volunteers. In January 1900, he was promoted to brigadier general in the regular army. In September 1906, he was promoted to lieutenant general.

The following account is of his action during the Battle of Chattanooga for which he received the Medal of Honor, the nation's highest award for valor.

TRENCH: A ditch used for concealment and protection in warfare.

General Arthur MacArthur with his Medal of Honor earned in the attack on Missionary Ridge.
(National Archives)

Missionary Ridge. Grant's orders were for Thomas's men to seize only the rifle pits at the base of the ridge—and go no farther. Thomas passed these orders on to General Philip Sheridan, commander of the units assigned for the assault.

On November 25, 1863, just after 4 P.M., 18,000 men from the Army of the Cumberland, including the 24th Wisconsin, attacked. They soon were able to overwhelm the Confederate troops in the trenches and seize their objective. Now the Union troops were stuck in exposed positions where Confederate troops above were able to shoot point-blank into the milling Union ranks. The situation was rapidly becoming desperate. If the men stayed where they were, they'd be slaughtered. If they retreated, it would be another humiliating defeat, a defeat made worse because it would occur in full view of Generals Grant, Thomas, and others who were watching the action from nearby Orchard Knob. So, instead of rushing back to Chattanooga in a panic, there occurred what historians later called "one of the most dramatic moves in the entire war." Angry at the enemy fire and eager to erase the shame of the earlier defeat at Chickamauga, the Union troops seized the initiative and, without orders, began a pell-mell charge up the ridge.

When Grant saw what was happening, he turned to Thomas and asked angrily, "Thomas, who ordered those men up the ridge?" Thomas, equally startled, said he had no idea—he certainly hadn't. Grant turned to another senior officer with him, General Gordon Granger and demanded, "Did you order them up?" Granger replied, "No, they started up without orders." Grant was still unhappy, but there was nothing he could do about it. As he saw the blue-clad men scramble up the steep ridge he muttered, "Well, it will be all right if it turns out all right."

Meanwhile, it seemed as if the men of the Army of the Cumberland were in a race with one another to be the first to reach the crest of the ridge. Battle flags were important symbols of inspiration and unit pride for the troops. Men regarded it a high honor to be chosen to be a color-bearer—a person assigned to carry the battle flag. It was also considered a great honor for the unit and the individual involved if a soldier was successful in capturing an enemy's battle flag. Great glory would come to the first unit that could successfully plant its colors at the crest of the ridge. The battle flags from approximately 60 units were adding bobbing and waving accents of brilliant color to the surging mass of blue fighting up the ridge.

One of the men in the forefront of the charge was Captain Arthur MacArthur. MacArthur was beside the 24th Wisconsin's color-bearer when the man was hit in the head by a cannonball. MacArthur grabbed the flag from the dead soldier, waved it high, and shouted, "On Wisconsin!" Although few could have heard him above the sound of musket and cannon fire, they would have been able to see MacArthur wav-

The original Medal of Honor. Note that the medallion from this Civil War design, with modification, is used in the modern Navy and Marine Corps versions. (National Archives)

41

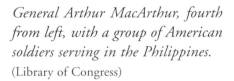

General Arthur MacArthur, fourth from left, with a group of American soldiers serving in the Philippines.
(Library of Congress)

ing the flag as he ran forward over the steep, broken ground. Inspired by their captain's example, the men of the 24th ran, stumbled, fought, and fell as they followed him in an effort to be the first to seize and hold the crest.

Before the sun set and in a dramatic silhouette against the sky, Captain MacArthur reached the crest and proudly plunged the base of the flagpole of the 24th Wisconsin into the ground. Other Union colors quickly followed as the Union troops consolidated their position. The Confederates fled from the ridge, and the siege of Chattanooga was ended.

Shortly after his troops took the ridge, General Sheridan arrived. He found MacArthur exhausted, his face blackened from smoke, his uniform torn and bloodstained. Sheridan embraced MacArthur, telling the men around them, "Take care of him. He has just won the Medal of Honor."

Captain E. B. Parsons, the senior captain in the 24th, later wrote to MacArthur's father saying, "Arthur was magnificent. . . . He has become the hero of the regiment. As you know, vacancies among the officers are now filled by vote, and Arthur, by unanimous agreement, has been elevated to the rank of Major."

MacArthur went on to become the commanding officer of the 24th Wisconsin. During the Battle of Atlanta in 1864, at age nineteen, MacArthur was breveted colonel, thus earning the nickname the "boy colonel."

Detail of a contemporary illustration of the Battle of Missionary Ridge. (Author's Collection)

IF YOU'D LIKE TO DISCOVER MORE

The nineteenth century was an extraordinary period in our nation's history. During that time, our nation acquired almost all the territory it has today and faced its greatest challenges. It was also a time of great heroes, among them Lee, Grant, and Jackson all who became famous during the American Civil War. Here is a short list of a books about these men and this period. Your library will have many more.

Custer and Crazy Horse by Stephen E. Ambrose
A House Divided: The Lives of Ulysses S. Grant and Robert E. Lee by Jules Archer
The Civil War A to Z by Norman Bolotin
The Mexican War: Mr. Polk's War by Charles W. Carey
Scholastic Encyclopedia of the Civil War by Catherine Clinton
Stonewall by Jean Fritz
Fields of Fury by James M. McPherson
The Boys' War by Jim Murphy
Civil War Battles and Leaders Edited by Aaron R. Murray
The Class of 1846 by John C. Waugh

Chapter

3

EMERGING AS A WORLD POWER

1899~1937

PHILIPPINE INSURRECTION

The conflict known as the Philippine Insurrection had its origin in the Spanish-American War. That war was caused by American sympathy for the Cuban nationalist insurrection against Spanish colonial rule that started in 1895 and by the mysterious destruction of the battleship USS *Maine* in Havana Harbor on February 15, 1898, which was blamed on the Spanish. Secretary of State John Hay called the Spanish-American War "a splendid little war." It was brief, lasting from April 21–August 12, 1898. There were fewer than 400 American battle casualties, and at its conclusion, the United States acquired an empire. Peace negotiations between the United States and Spain resulted in the Treaty of Paris of 1898 that formally ended hostilities. By the terms of the treaty, Spain received $20 million from the United States, Cuba gained its independence, and the United States received possession of the Spanish colonies of Guam, Puerto Rico, and the Philippines. Philippine nationalists, who had been fighting for independence from

Spain since 1896, were outraged. Even though President William McKinley promised the Filipino people political and social reforms and a U.S. policy of "benevolent assimilation," the Filipino nationalists would have none of it.

On January 21, 1899, the nationalists declared an independent Philippine Republic with Emilio Aguinaldo as its president. For the rest of the year the Filipinos waged conventional warfare against U.S. troops. Although the Filipino troops fought bravely, they were poorly armed and poorly led. By February 1900, U.S. forces had captured every major city in the Philippine archipelago. When President Aguinaldo saw that his men could not defeat American troops in formal battle, he proclaimed a policy of continued resistance through "guerilla warfare."

President Aguinaldo went into hiding, and the war degenerated into a series of harassment attacks and ambushes led by fiercely independent regional chieftains and warlords. The most tenacious of the insurrectionists were the Moros, Filipino Muslim tribes that inhabited the southern Philippine Islands. The Moros were fierce warriors that were regarded as atrocity-committing barbarians by the Spanish. American troops would quickly discover how tenacious and deadly the Moros were. Moros were not above using terror tactics to keep their autonomy. They typically butchered any enemy soldier or administrator they captured, leaving the slaughtered remains as a warning for others. During the next two years, U.S. troops embarked on a series of campaigns that ultimately broke the back of the guerrillas' power. On July 4, 1902, President Theodore Roosevelt officially declared the "insurrection" over. Sporadic fighting and incidents of violent unrest remained a chronic problem for U.S. authorities, and did would not end until 1913. The Philippines finally became an independent nation on July 4, 1946.

 ## MEXICAN EXPEDITIONS

When World War I began in Europe in 1914, the United States quickly announced that it would remain neutral. Though the Atlantic Ocean protected it from the conflict in Europe, the United States found itself facing a potential threat from Mexico. In 1914, Mexico was in a state of anarchy. The government under the dictator Porfirio Díaz, had collapsed and a brief and violent power struggle erupted between his former subordinates. Later that year, General Venustiano Carranza emerged as the head of a new Mexican government recognized by the United States. But Carranza's government was weak and faction-ridden, and he had almost no control over the regional leaders he had defeated for the presidency of Mexico. Matters were made worse by Germany which offered military assistance to Mexico if it promised to declare war on the United States. Germany believed that if it could involve the United States in a war with Mexico, it would be too busy to come to the aid of Great Britain and France. A telegram detailing Germany's plans, later known as the Zimmermann Telegram, was intercepted by Great Britain in 1917 and given to the United States. The Zimmermann telegram created a scandal that ultimately caused the United States to declare war on Germany. Before that, President Woodrow Wilson ordered two expeditions into Mexico to ensure the peace along its southern border. The first was the Expedition to Veracruz in 1914, and the second was the Punitive Expedition from 1916 to 1917.

Veracruz was Mexico's largest port, and the historic gateway to Mexico City. The United States seized the port with the dual purpose of preventing German weapons and ammunition from being delivered to Mexico and positioning it to serve as a staging area for a possible campaign to Mexico City. A diplomatic agreement was soon reached in which Mexico promised not to wage war against the U.S. and the troops were withdrawn.

The more famous of the two expeditions by far was the Punitive Expedition against the Mexican border raider Pancho Villa. For Americans, Francisco "Pancho" Villa was the most famous of the regional Mexican leaders. His power base was in the north, along the U.S./Mexico border. He and his men repeatedly crossed the border and raided and terrorized towns from Arizona to Texas. Though he was a bandit and an out-and-out thief, Villa was also a charismatic leader with a brilliant sense of self-promotion. Once, he discovered that a raid he had planned was scheduled to occur during the World Series. Realizing news of his raid would be competing for front-page newspaper space with baseball's championship event Villa postponed it until after the World Series was over, saying to his men, "We shall hold off the attack, boys, until the Americans finish their ball games."

He succeeded in capturing the imagination of Americans not affected by his raids by presenting himself as a liberator of the Mexican peasants and as something of a Hispanic Robin Hood—although in his case he robbed from the rich and lavishly gave to himself and his top lieutenants.

The publicity gave Pancho Villa a certain glamorous aura, but his raids on American ranches, mines, and border towns spread panic in the region and demands for President Woodrow Wilson to do something to stop them. After repeated peaceful attempts failed to end Villa's incursions, President Wilson in 1916 ordered Brigadier General John J. Pershing to assemble an army and embark on a "punitive expedition" to capture Villa "dead or alive." The Mexican Border Campaign—popularly called the "Punitive Expedition"—would prove a failure. Villa was never captured. Pershing, sensitive to Mexican feelings about the incursion into their land, conducted the invasion, with great tact. Even so, it caused widespread resentment throughout Mexico. When it became obvious that Villa would never be captured, the U.S. and Mexican governments reached a face-saving diplomatic agreement in January 1917, and the troops were recalled. The last U.S. soldiers left Mexico on February 5, 1917.

Although the campaign did not attain its stated goal of capturing Villa, the episode was not totally a waste. The American army gained invaluable administrative and field experience that would be put to use later that year on the battlefields of France when the United States joined the Allied side against Germany in World War I.

 **WORLD WAR I**

When the Great War (as it was originally called) began on July 28, 1914, most people believed that the conflict between the Central Powers of Imperial Germany, Austria-Hungary, and the Ottoman Empire (composed primarily of Turkey and the Middle East) and the Allies of Great Britain, France, Italy, and Imperial Russia, would be over in a matter of weeks, if not months. No one, even the dourest of pessimists, imagined that it would last four years and cost millions of lives.

The United States managed to remain neutral for most of the war. A series of provocations by Imperial Germany, including unrestricted submarine warfare against passenger and cargo ships and, the Zimmermann Telegram affair, forced President Woodrow Wilson to request Congress to declare war on April 6, 1917.

When World War I concluded at 11:00 A.M. on November 11, 1918—the "eleventh hour of the eleventh day of the eleventh month"—eight million soldiers lay dead and twenty million more were wounded. Twenty-two million civilians had been killed or wounded, and the map of Europe was in the process of being redrawn. By 1919, four great royal empires—Imperial Germany, Austria-Hungary, Imperial Russia, and the Ottoman Empire—were no more. In their place were the new nations of Finland, Estonia, Latvia, Lithuania, Czechoslovakia, Austria, Hungary, Yugoslavia, Turkey, Syria, Mesopotamia, Arabia, and Palestine. After more than a century, Poland, whose territory had been carved up among Germany, Russia, and Austria-Hungary in 1795 in the Third Partition of Poland, was once again a sovereign nation. Kaiser Wilhelm II of Germany had abdicated the throne and gone into exile in the Netherlands. Germany was now a republic.

The most traumatic change occurred in Russia. In 1917, its ruler Czar Nicholas II abdicated. In 1918, he and his family were shot dead by assassins. A new communist government led by the Bolshevik Vladimir Ilyich Lenin seized control of the nation in 1917, proclaimed a new republic named the Union of Soviet Socialist Republics, and announced a world communist revolution whose purpose was to overthrow the "corrupt capitalist democracies" of the West.

World War I would have a tremendous impact on the careers of John Pershing, Douglas MacArthur, George Marshall, George Patton, Dwight Eisenhower, and Maurice Rose. As the commanding general of the American Expeditionary Force, Pershing would reach the pinnacle of his career. MacArthur would earn his brigadier general's star and become a hero leading the 42nd "Rainbow" Division, so named because it was composed of men from almost every state in the Union. Patton would gain fame and invaluable experience as the leader of the army's first tank unit. Marshall would hone staff skills that would serve him well as Army Chief of Staff in the larger and more demanding World War II. The high-pressure training program overseen by Eisenhower in camps in the United States exposed him to young Americans from across the nation. He emerged from that experience with a realization that the American man, with no tradition of war, could learn the brutal skills necessary to wage war, and win it. It was a knowledge that would, in World War II as the commander of Supreme Headquarters Allied Expeditionary Force (SHAEF), give him confidence in victory during the war's darkest days. Teenage Maurice Rose found his calling as an officer in the army in the training and trenches of World War I.

When it concluded, World War I was called "the war to end all wars." The Treaty of Versailles that formally ended the war was signed in 1919. When French field marshal Ferdinand Foch read it, he saw that it was more a document of punishment against Germany than a peace treaty. He claimed that the Allies had only bought "twenty years" of peace. Foch died in 1929; thus, he did not see his uncannily accurate prediction come true when, in 1939, World War II in Europe erupted.

 ## CARIBBEAN CONFLICTS

The Caribbean conflicts, sometimes called the "Banana Wars" after one of the main cash crops in the region, were a series of insurgency outbreaks in the Caribbean and Nicaragua that began in 1914 and ended in 1933. A limited amount of American troops, mostly Marines, assisted the governments of Haiti, the Dominican Republic, and Nicaragua to help suppress insurrection movements.

Haiti was particularly hard hit by the guerilla conflict. A poor country that shares the Caribbean island of Hispaniola with the Dominican Republic, it had suffered a series of revolutions since 1914. In 1916 the shaky government requested military assistance from the United States to help police the country and combat the rebel Cacos. These fierce tribesmen conducted terror campaigns against the government and populace that were so bold that at its height not even government ministries in the capital city of Port-au-Prince were safe from attack. The Caco campaign ended in May 1920, when two important chieftains, Charlemagne Peralta and Benoit Baterville, were killed by Marine-led patrols. The Haitian government declared an armistice to Cacos who would surrender their weapons and honor the peace. As an added incentive, each Caco who did so would receive new clothing and ten dollars, a considerable sum in poverty-stricken Haiti. Hundreds of Cacos responded and very quickly the Caco insurrection was over.

 **INTERWAR YEARS**

The 23 years between the end of World War I and the beginning of World War II were among the most traumatic for the U.S. military services. After the Allied victory in World War I, the United States returned to its tradition of isolationism and a small, peacetime military. Rapid demobilization of the armed forces occurred. In 1918 the army had a peak strength of 3.7 million men. When the National Defense Act of 1920 was passed by Congress, the army was authorized a maximum of 200,000 men. In 1921, Congress reduced the ranks to 150,000 men. In 1922, a further cut to 137,000 men was made, a level sustained until 1936. The United States went from one of the largest military powers to one ranked seventeenth in the world.

The national economic collapse of the Great Depression of the 1930s resulted in an additional succession of military budgetary cutbacks. Branches, such as the new Tank Corps, were eliminated because of their expense. Many military units became "phantom commands," existing only on paper. Promotions were frozen and officers, including Marshall, Patton, Eisenhower, Rose, and others who had distinguished themselves in World War I, found themselves demoted to prewar ranks. Many remained in those reduced ranks for years. The cutbacks reached rock bottom shortly after the election of President Franklin D. Roosevelt in 1932. In 1934, President Roosevelt met with Secretary of War George Dearn and Army Chief of Staff General Douglas MacArthur. The War Department budget was going to be reduced from $277 million to $197 million; and Roosevelt told MacArthur that the army's portion of the budget would be cut by 51 percent. MacArthur was so outraged that he could not contain himself. He told the president, "When we lose the next war, and an American boy with an enemy bayonet through his belly and an enemy foot on his dying throat spits out his last curse, I want the name not to be MacArthur, but Roosevelt." MacArthur was certain he would be fired, because the last thing anyone does is lose his temper and yell at the president. But Roosevelt kept him, and did not reduce the budget. Secretary Dearn later claimed that MacArthur's outburst had "saved the army."

The Air Corps, as it was then known, was administratively a part of the army. It, too, suffered from the budget cutbacks. Attempts to create an independent air force during this time failed, and it was not until after World War II in 1947 that the independent U.S. Air Force would be created. In order to survive during the Twenties and Thirties, the Air Corps exploited the enthusiasm the public had for aviation by staging a number of events that would bring the Air Corps favorable, often front-page, publicity. These included record-setting endurance, speed, and distance feats.

Japan's invasion of China and Nazi Germany's rearmament in the 1930s ended the cutbacks of the military. For the next few years the budgets would slowly increase for all the services. With the Japanese sneak attack on Pearl Harbor on December 7, 1941, the inter-war years came to a dramatic end. The United States returned to the world stage as a major military power.

 **SECOND SINO-JAPANESE WAR**

Three regional conflicts preceded the conflict that became World War II. They were the invasion of Abyssinia (present-day Ethiopia) by the army of Fascist Italy in 1935, the Spanish Civil War in 1936 in which Nazi Germany helped forces led by General Francisco Franco seize control of Spain, and the Second Sino-Japanese War launched on July 7, 1937. The Second Sino-Japanese War was an invasion of eastern China by Japan. Militarily more powerful than the Chinese, the Imperial Japanese Army and Navy waged a successful campaign that occupied the major ports of Shanghai, Nanking, Nanjing, and the surrounding territory . One of the most famous and shocking photos of this war was the photograph of a terrified baby surrounded by bombed wreckage in a Shanghai rail yard.

The United States was neutral at this time. Because there were many Americans living and working in China, a small force of marines as well as some navy ships were sent to protect U.S. citizens and, whenever possible, observe Japanese military activities. After the Japanese attack on U.S. military facilities at Pearl Harbor, Hawaii, on December 7, 1941, this war became a part of the larger World War II. When the United States entered World War II, it sent military aid to the nationalist Chinese forces lead by Chiang Kai-shek to help the Chinese fight the Japanese. Though the aid did keep China in the war, defeat of Japan in 1945 came from independent U.S. campaigns in the Pacific Ocean.

JOHN J. PERSHING *The Muslim Guerillas*

The Spanish-American War was one of the shortest armed conflicts in American military history. Although it lasted less than four months its impact was enormous. The United States went to war against Spain in the spring of 1898 in order to help Cuba, then a Spanish territory, gain its independence. When the peace treaty was signed on August 12, 1898, the United States also found itself in possession of a new empire that included the islands of Puerto Rico, Guam, and the Philippines. The Philippines had been in revolt against Spain at the same time as Cuba. When the Philippine rebels learned that their country would not get independence as well, they launched a rebellion against the United States that came to be called the Philippine Insurrection. Captain John Pershing arrived at the Philippines in 1900, a time when the rebellion against American rule had largely ended. The exception was in the south, in and around the Philippine island of Mindanao, where the fierce Muslim tribes known as Moros lived.

The warlike Moros were skilled in piracy and banditry. For six centuries they had dominated the seas from the island of Borneo in the south to the Philippines. They jealously defended their religious customs and homes with a barbaric savagery. A few Moro tribes accommodated themselves to Spanish and, later, American authority. Most tribes, though, fiercely fought off any attempt of Spanish rule and saw no reason to change their ways and accept American authority. Subduing these warlike tribes would be difficult. Many in the region thought it would be impossible.

Initially, Pershing was posted to a staff position in the Department of Mindanao and Jolo, which was responsible for keeping order in the area. Unlike most of his fellow officers who, when off duty, would lounge on the beach and be attended by Filipino servants, Pershing spent his free time studying the Moros and their customs. He learned to speak a number of the Moro dialects and to read Arabic. He studied the Koran. He honed his lessons by practicing what he learned with the few friendly Moro tribes that inhabited the coast of Mindanao.

Biography in Brief
JOHN JOSEPH "BLACK JACK" PERSHING (1860-1948) fought in the Spanish-American War (1898), the Philippine Insurrection (1899-1903), the Punitive Expedition (1916-1917), and World War I (1914-1918). Pershing graduated from West Point in 1886. He served with distinction in the Spanish-American War and in the Philippine Insurrection. On Sept. 20, 1906, Captain Pershing was promoted to brigadier general by President Theodore Roosevelt.

Appointed commander of the American Expeditionary Force (AEF) in World War I, ultimately composed of more than 2 million men, he commanded the largest American army up to that time. Pershing led the American troops in the decisive Meuse-Argonne Offensive that secured Allied victory against Germany in 1918. By an Act of Congress on September 8, 1919, Pershing became the first soldier to hold the rank of General of the Armies of the United States. Pershing died in 1948 at Walter Reed Army Medical Center.

The following event recounts a crucial moment during his service in the Philippine Insurrection, one that resulted in his receiving an honor unique in American military history.

Captain John Pershing (National Archives)

Pershing later wrote an assessment of the Moros, noting, "The almost infinite combination of superstitions, prejudices and suspicions blended with his character make him a difficult person to handle until fully understood. In order to control him other than by brute force, one must first win his implicit confidence." Pershing received the opportunity to put his observations into action on June 30, 1902, when he was made commander of the 700-man Camp Vicars located near Lake Lanao in northwestern Mindanao.

Most American army officers stationed in the Philippines viewed the Moros as savages to be kept at arm's distance—

Pershing's boyhood home in Laclede, Linn County, Missouri. (Library of Congress)

ignored if peaceful or punished if warlike. Pershing was different. He chose to deal with the Moros as fellow human beings. Because he took the time to learn their customs, Pershing had discovered that they were passionate chess players. Whenever the opportunity arose, Pershing would enter into a match with a local Moro datoo, or chief. The game was generally played out in the open and Pershing would squat on the ground opposite the datoo and play chess for hours. Many of the tribes under his authority responded favorably to Pershing's diplomacy and signed peace treaties. But several tribes refused. It became obvious to him that he would have to use force to bring these rebellious tribes in line.

Recognizing that any military action on his part would be regarded with suspicion by the Moro tribes he had signed peace treaties with, Pershing made a point of first reassuring these tribes that they had nothing to fear from him or his men. That done, on September 28, 1902, he took a force of several hundred men containing cavalry, infantry, artillery, and engineers and embarked on a campaign to subdue the tribes starting with the powerful Sultan of Maciu, leader of the most

Pershing got the name "Black Jack" because he commanded African-American troops known as "Buffalo Soldiers" when he was stationed in Montana in the late 1800s. It later also came to describe his stern way of dealing with adversaries.

A commemorative stamp of John Pershing. Note that there are four general's stars on his epaulet.
(Author's collection)

STORM: In the military, a sudden, strong, usually overwhelming attack.

intransigent of the rebellious tribes.

The Sultan's fort was located at the tip of a narrow, swampy peninsula on Lake Lanao. The fort had tall walls that were ten feet thick. Surrounding the fort was a moat. Pershing had two choices: cross the swamp or bring boats through the jungle and attack the fort from the lake. Pershing chose to attack from the land. He ordered his engineers to construct a road through the swamp using trees cut from the surrounding jungle. This project took almost two weeks to complete. Then Pershing positioned his men in assault lines facing the fort and brought up his artillery. Pershing then called upon the Sultan to surrender, but the Sultan refused, defiantly unfurling his red battle flags.

Storming a well-defended fort usually means that the attacking force will suffer heavy casualties, but Pershing had a plan he was sure would bring him victory with very few casualties. The first part of the plan was launched on the afternoon of October 11 with an artillery attack. As the shells smashed into the fort, a newspaper correspondent accompanying the force asked Pershing, "Will you storm the fort tonight?"

"No, we would lose too many men," Pershing answered.

"But aren't you afraid [the Moros] will sneak out . . . during the night and get away?" asked the reporter.

"That's just what I expect them to do," Pershing said.

When dusk arrived, Pershing ordered the artillery bombardment to stop. Then he told his men to prepare for a night attack by the Moros. That evening, just as Pershing predicted, howling Moros armed with rifles, wavy-bladed krises, cleaver-like barongs, two-handed swords called campilans, and bolos, attacked. American troops fired volley after volley into the Moro ranks. The attack wavered, then broke and the Moros retreated, carrying their wounded with them.

The following day, not a sound was heard from inside the fort. Warily the American troops approached the fort's walls. Suddenly a handful of fanatic defenders armed with barongs rushed out toward the troops and were quickly cut down. When Pershing and his men entered the stronghold, they discovered it was deserted. During the night the survivors had quietly escaped over the water. The Moros were a people who greatly respected military skill. This victory proved a tremendous boost to Pershing's already favorable reputation with them.

Not long after his defeat of the Sultan of Maciu, a cholera epidemic broke out in the region and within a few weeks about 1,500 natives had died of the disease. Pershing obtained medicines and instructions for their use and had them distributed to the areas hardest hit.

Although Pershing had built up a lot of good will at this point, he found himself continually being tested. At about the same time of the cholera epidemic, another powerful Moro datoo, the Sultan of Bayan, began making threats that he would wage war against the Americans. Pershing called the Sultan's bluff, saying that he would immediately organize another military expedition. The sultan promptly backed down, saying that he would visit Pershing at Camp Vicars to discuss a peace. The sultan and his court arrived shortly thereafter. The sultan was dressed in brightly colored clothing that included tight red pants with gold buttons down the side. The meeting was going well, when at one point Pershing surprised the sultan by announcing that he would "return your compliment by visiting you." The sultan was dismayed. The last thing he wanted was this leader of the Americans in the middle of his fort, but Pershing, thanks to his awareness of the Moro's code of hospitality, had neatly trapped the sultan.

Within weeks, Pershing, at the head of an escort of infantry and a battery of artillery, appeared in front of the Sultan of Bayan's fort. The fort had no gate, so Pershing and some of his men had to clamber over the wall on ladders. Once inside, Pershing raised the American flag over the fort and ordered a 21-gun salute to be fired. As Pershing suspected, the Moros were impressed with the booming artillery. The sultan was so impressed that he asked Pershing to become the adopted father of his wife, an offer that soon extended to four children of the tribe as well.

As the visit continued, the sultan and his court reached

Philippine patriot Emilio Aguinado. (U.S. Army)

55

A Moro Datto, left center, with his children and in the company of U.S. soldiers and Philippine civilians. (National Archives)

Pershing possessed one lifetime habit not even the military could erase: tardiness. Once, during World War I, he was late meeting the King and Queen of Belgium. The reason: he couldn't get his boots on!

an unprecedented decision. They told Pershing that they wished to consecrate him as a datoo "by the law and rites of the Koran," making him a tribal chieftain, blood relative, and counselor of the Moros of Bayan. It was an extraordinary honor that had never before been offered to a Christian. Pershing promptly accepted.

In an account of the Muslim ceremony, Pershing later wrote, "Each sultan and datoo, with his prominent followers in his rear, sat on his heels, the whole forming a circle. The sacred Koran was placed on a mat of native fiber in the center of this circle, guarded by an aged Mohammedan priest, gorgeous in trousers of all colors and a yellow silk upper garment, over whose head a slave held a beautiful silk sunshade. Silver boxes, beautifully engraved, containing betel nut were passed around the circle and then the speechmaking began, each chief in turn giving his opinion. . . . At the conclusion, all the rulers and myself, placing our hands upon the Koran, registered a vow of eternal friendship, allegiance to the United States, and agreed upon a cessation of warfare against each other."

Pershing was now the U.S. Army's first—and only—datoo. An editorial in the Manila Times praised Pershing for "having won the submission of Bayan through diplomacy" and, in becoming a datoo, receiving a "distinction never before enjoyed by an American."

Pershing would have further challenges in Mindanao and would have to wage another campaign against other rebellious tribes in order to achieve peace in his region. Pershing's actions had made him famous back in the United States. He had also impressed his superiors. At that time the president's cabinet contained two departments responsible for defense, the Department of War, responsible for all military matters having to do with armies, and the Department of the Navy. Elihu Root the Secretary of War, wrote to Pershing's commanding officer, General S. S. Sumner, asking him, "Express to Captain Pershing and officers and men under his command the thanks of the War Department for their able and effective

accomplishment of a difficult and important task." When he returned to Washington, D.C., later in 1902, Pershing was introduced by President Theodore Roosevelt to his guests as "our leading military fighter."

An artillery piece fires at guerilla positions. (U.S. Army)

General John Pershing, commanding general, American Expeditionary Force in World War I. (National Archives)

57

GEORGE C. MARSHALL *The Crocodile Scare*

Biography in Brief

GEORGE CATLETT MARSHALL (1880-1959) participated in the Philippine Insurrection (1899-1903), World War I (1914-1918), and World War II (1939-1945). He graduated from Virginia Military Institute and was commissioned a second lieutenant in the army on February 3, 1902. He was promoted to captain in 1916. In World War I, as a staff officer in the AEF, he distinguished himself with his organizational and planning ability.

On September 1, 1939, the same day that Nazi Germany invaded Poland to start World War II in Europe, Marshall, then a brigadier general, was appointed Chief of Staff of the U. S. Army and promoted to the rank of general. Marshall was Army Chief of Staff during World War II, responsible for expanding the army from 200,000 to 8,000,000 soldiers and directing a global war campaign. On December 16, 1944, he was promoted to General of the Army.

On January 21, 1947, he became Secretary of State. During his tenure the European Recovery Program, or Marshall Plan, designed to restore war-devastated Europe, was enacted. He resigned in January 1949. From September 1950 to September 1951 he was Secretary of Defense. In December 1953, he was awarded the Nobel Peace Prize. On October 16, 1959, Marshall died at the Walter Reed Army Medical Center.

This account is from his tour of duty in the Philippines.

George C. Marshall was a newly commissioned second lieutenant in 1902 when he was ordered to the Philippines. At the time the Philippines was one of the most remote and primitive outposts in the U.S. military. For many officers it was regarded as the worst posting one could receive. It was not unusual for an officer who had connections to try and get reassigned. But Marshall had no such connections. As he later noted, "There isn't anything much lower than a second lieutenant and I was about the junior second lieutenant in the Army at that time."

The Philippine Insurrection was in its final days when Marshall arrived for duty at the garrison stationed in Calapan, the capital city of the island of Mindoro. Sporadic fighting between unorganized guerillas and American garrison forces was a danger, but less of a threat than boredom, tropical disease, and low morale.

Although he was new to both uniform and command, Marshall was a fast learner, and he was also smart enough to listen and learn from the more experienced men in the unit. His attitude so impressed his commanding officer that within two weeks of his arrival at Mindoro, Marshall was given command of a company of men, and in July 1902 he was made acting civil governor for the southern part of Mindoro. Marshall proved diligent with his new administrative duties as well as his field responsibilities.

Although Marshall's conduct and performance had been extraordinary, he still had less then one year's experience as a commissioned officer in the Army. One of Marshall's many responsibilities was to search for guerillas in the region under his authority. It was during one of these patrols that he encountered the first real test to his authority and leadership ability.

A group of bandits had been reported on a small island nearby. Upon receiving the news, Marshall promptly took seven men on a boat to the island to investigate. After they landed, the patrol passed through a village where they saw a

George Marshall was a rarity among the top generals in that he did not attend the U.S. Military Academy at West Point. He was a graduate of the Virginia Military Institute (VMI).

General of the Army George C. Marshall (AP/Wide World)

group of natives sewing up a pony that had recently been bitten by a crocodile. With this vivid reminder of one of the many natural dangers that inhabit the Philippines, the soldiers cautiously proceeded into the jungle.

Soon they encountered a narrow, deep stream that they had to cross. With Marshall in the lead, the squad began to ford the stream. All the men were in the water when a splash was heard. One of the more nervous men shouted, "Crocodile!" In a panic, the men in the squad surged and thrashed forward,

George Marshal in World War I, shortly after he was promoted to colonel. (National Archives)

GUERILLA: A member of an irregular military force operating in small bands in occupied terrritory to conduct hit-and-run raids against an enemy.

knocking the surprised Marshall into the bank and trampling him into the mud as they ran headlong over him and onto the shore.

Marshall picked himself up and, thoroughly soaked and covered with mud, strode over to his men. He realized that unless he was able to reassert his command over his men, he would be useless as an officer. As he later said, he decided that this "wasn't a time for cussing around." Instead, using his ringing drill-sergeant strong voice, he ordered his men to fall in, shoulder their rifles, and face the river they had just crossed. Marshall then took the lead and gave the order for them to march. Down the men went, following their lieutenant into the stream. When they emerged on the other side, Marshall ordered them to turn around. Once again he led them through the "crocodile-infested" water.

When they arrived on the other side again, Marshall said, "I halted them, faced them toward me, inspected their rifles, and then [dismissed them]." Discipline had been restored. This was a story that Marshall would tell with great enjoyment for the rest of his life.

Soldiers from a Kansas unit stationed in the Philippines during the Philippine Insurrection. (Library of Congress)

A Moro tribe family with some American soldiers. (National Archives)

DOUGLAS MacARTHUR *A Special Operations Mission at Veracruz*

Biography in Brief

DOUGLAS MacARTHUR (1880-1964), son of General Arthur MacArthur, participated in the Philippine Insurrection (1899-1903), the Veracruz Expedition (1914), World War I (1914-1918), World War II (1939-1945), and the Korean War (1950-1953). He graduated from West Point in 1903.

In World War I, on June 26, 1918, MacArthur was promoted to brigadier general. In 1919, he became the superintendent at West Point. In 1930, he was appointed Army Chief of Staff and promoted to the rank of general. In 1935 he was sent to the Philippines with orders to organize its military defenses prior to the country's independence from the United States.

During World War II, he conducted the campaign against the Japanese in the southwest Pacific. He was promoted to General of the Army in 1944. After the war, he was Supreme Commander for the Allied Powers (SCAP), responsible for the postwar administration of Japan.

During the Korean War, MacArthur commanded the United Nations military forces. A dispute in strategy with President Harry S Truman caused MacArthur's relief on April 11, 1951. MacArthur returned to the United States and ran unsuccessfully against Dwight Eisenhower, a former aide, for the 1952 Republican nomination for president. MacArthur died in New York City in 1964.

This event recounts his secret mission during the Veracruz Expedition for which he was recommended for the Medal of Honor.

On April 21, 1914, President Wilson received a message that Germany—a country that would in four short months help plunge Europe into World War I—was shipping military supplies to Mexico. To stop that shipment from reaching the hostile Mexican government, Wilson ordered U.S. troops to occupy Veracruz, Mexico's largest port. For the second time in less than 70 years, American forces under the command of Brigadier General Frederick Funston followed in the steps of General Winfield Scott and captured Veracruz. Captain Douglas MacArthur assumed he would soon be going to war, serving on the staff of Major General Leonard Wood, but General Wood had something more important in mind for the handsome, 34-year-old captain.

A Mexican army of about 11,000 troops surrounded General Funston and his command of 7,000 men at Veracruz. In addition, Mexican rebels, who were also anti-American, freely roamed the countryside making patrolling a highly hazardous undertaking. Funston's orders allowed him to repel any attack, but otherwise he was to remain on the defensive and hold the city. He was even forbidden to patrol outside the city walls. Meanwhile, in Washington, D.C., Major General Leonard Wood received his orders. He was to prepare a top secret assault on Mexico City if a diplomatic settlement regarding the shipment of weapons from Germany could not be reached.

Historically, Veracruz is the gateway to Mexico City. It was at Veracruz in 1519 that Hernando Cortez and his conquistadors landed and began their conquest of Mexico. In 1847 it was at Veracruz that the U.S. Army under General Winfield Scott landed and embarked on the conquest of Mexico. Now again, U.S. troops were in Mexico and poised to march in the footsteps of their grandfathers, but for the assault on Mexico City to succeed, General Wood needed information about the area and defenses around Veracruz. In what today would be called a special operations mission, General Wood turned to a member of his staff, Captain Douglas MacArthur, and ordered him to embark on a dangerous and top secret mission to Veracruz as a special intelligence agent. Wood's orders were for MacArthur "to obtain through reconnaissance . . . all possible information which would be of value in connection with [the advance to Mexico City]."

MacArthur arrived at Veracruz on May 1, 1914, and reported to General Funston and explained that he would be working outside of Funston's command. The importance of keeping MacArthur's mission secret was paramount. Not even Funston was made aware of the details of MacArthur's mission. If the Mexican government discovered his purpose, they would immediately attack and overwhelm Funston's force before reinforcements could arrive.

Road conditions were primitive at that time. Considering the wealth of heavy equipment and supplies that the Americans would have to transport in support of an offensive on Mexico City, Captain Constant Cordier, an infantry officer at Veracruz, later wrote, "with the rainy season on, it would have been well-nigh impossible . . . without using the railroad for our advance." This presented a problem for the Americans because, as Captain Cordier noted, "We had ample [railroad cars] but no engines."

On May 6, MacArthur learned of the possible existence of locomotives in Alvarado, a town about 40 miles southeast from Veracruz. If this information was correct, Alvarado would be of enormous strategic importance to the Americans, and capture of these locomotives would be the first objective of the offensive. MacArthur found three Mexicans in Veracruz with railroad experience, an engineer and two firemen, and offered them $150 in gold if they would help him find the locomotives. Fearing treachery, he told them they would only get the gold after he safely returned. In addition, he searched the engineer and took from him a pistol and a knife. Then MacArthur ordered the engineer to search him to show that MacArthur was not carrying any money and to underscore the fact that, if any of them did kill MacArthur, all they would get would be his pistol and clothing. MacArthur ordered the two firemen to leave in advance of his own departure in order to obtain handcars they would need to travel down the rail lines

West Point cadet Douglas MacArthur. (West Point Museum)

Captain Douglas MacArthur at Veracruz. (U.S. Army)

to Alvarado. Both parties would rendezvous at a rail intersection MacArthur was assured would not be under watch by the Mexican army.

At dusk on May 6, under the added protection of a rainstorm, MacArthur in uniform and the engineer quietly passed

Brigadier General Douglas MacArthur in France during World War I. (National Archives)

through the line of American outposts. They met the engineers at the rendezvous site and the four men rode the handcar to Alvarado. Outside the town they abandoned the handcar and, just after 1:00 A.M. on May 7, MacArthur arrived at the rail yard. There he found three engines that, he later reported, "were just what we needed—fine big road pullers in excellent condition except for a few minor parts which were missing."

General Douglas MacArthur in the Philippines during World War II.
(National Archives)

Satisfied with his discovery, he began the return trip.

So far MacArthur had been lucky in not being spotted. As the only armed member in the group, and carrying only a .38-calibre revolver, he would have been hard-pressed to fight his way through a superior force, which could mean as few as two men armed with rifles. On his return to Veracruz, that's just what he had to do—not once, but three times against armed bands of rebels.

The first incident occurred at the outskirts of Salinas. While quietly making their way around the town, five armed Mexicans discovered them and ordered the group to halt. MacArthur and his men immediately broke into a run, outdistancing three of their pursuers. As the other two neared, MacArthur turned and fired. The men went down, and his band successfully escaped the first encounter. The second incident occurred at the town of Piedra. Of this encounter, in his report to General Wood, MacArthur wrote: ". . . in a driving mist, we ran flush into about fifteen mounted men. . . . We were among them before I realized it and were immediately the center of a melee. I was knocked down by the rush of horsemen and had three bullet holes through my clothes."

Although the bullets had torn the uniform, somehow they had missed MacArthur. MacArthur returned fire and hit four of the horsemen, driving off the rest. One of the men in MacArthur's group was wounded in the shoulder, but not seriously. After bandaging the wound, the band now on the handcar proceeded north as fast as they could, but just before they reached American lines they met with trouble for the third time. Of it, MacArthur wrote in his report, "Near Laguna we were again encountered and fired upon by three mounted men who kept up a running fight with the hand car. I did not return this fire. All but one of these men was outdistanced, but . . . one man, unusually well mounted, overhauled and passed the car. He sent one bullet through my shirt and two others that hit the car within six inches of me, and I then felt obliged to bring him down."

MacArthur and his men reached American lines without further incident. Shortly thereafter, MacArthur returned to Washington, D.C., mission accomplished. In a separate report to General Wood, Captain Cordier wrote, "Knowing the out-lying conditions as well as I do it is a mystery to me that any of the party escaped." Furthermore, noting that the U.S. Navy had already awarded eleven Medals of Honor to its men for action at Veracruz, he recommended that MacArthur receive the Medal of Honor "for heroism displayed, for dangers braved, and for difficulties overcome." After he read MacArthur's report, Wood agreed, stating in his recommendation, "at a risk of his life" and "on his own initiative, [MacArthur showed] enterprise and courage worthy of high commendation." Unfortunately, the medal awards board rejected the recommendation, reducing the award to a lesser medal. MacArthur would finally receive the Medal of Honor in 1942 in the early years of World War II.

Funston and his troops remained at Veracruz for another seven months, when a diplomatic settlement between the United States and Mexico was reached in which Mexico promised not to go to war against the United States. The German arms never reached Mexico. Instead the merchant ship carrying them returned to Germany. As for Mexico and the United States, though tensions had eased temporarily they would flare up again in 1916 along the western U.S./Mexican border.

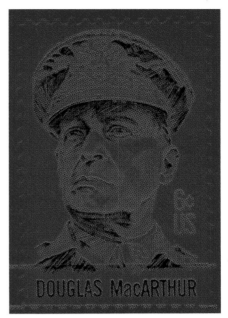

A stamp commemorating General of the Army Douglas MacArthur. (Author's collection)

GEORGE S. PATTON, Jr. *A Shoot-Out with Mexican Bandits*

Biography in Brief

GEORGE SMITH PATTON, JR. (1885-1945), fought in the Punitive Expedition (1916-1917), World War I (1914-1918), and World War II (1939-1945). Patton graduated from West Point in 1909. In World War I, Lieutenant Colonel Patton was the commander of the army's first tank unit. In October 1918, he was promoted to colonel. In 1920, following the reduction of the army, Patton reverted to his permanent rank of captain. He would not return to the rank of colonel until 1938. Patton was promoted to brigadier general on October 1, 1940. He rose rapidly in rank to general on April 14, 1945.

Patton achieved his greatest fame during World War II as a corps and army commander in North Africa and Europe. After Germany's defeat in May 1945, Patton was appointed military governor of the German province of Bavaria. He was relieved because of a political controversy later that year. On December 9, 1945, he suffered a broken neck in an automobile accident and died at a military hospital in Germany on December 21, 1945.

The following event recounts the exploit in the Punitive Expedition that made Patton a national hero.

In May, 1916, Lieutenant George S. Patton, Jr. was one of Brigadier General John Pershing's aides in the American Army's Punitive Expedition. The expedition had been ordered by President Woodrow Wilson to capture or kill the Mexican bandit leader Francisco "Pancho" Villa. It was a very frustrating time for the American troops. Despite the fact that the new inventions of the automobile and airplane gave them greater speed and mobility in their search, they had come up with nothing. The past several months had turned into a series of wild goose chases in the rugged Mexican wilderness south of the Rio Grande. Although his troops occasionally encountered and skirmished with isolated units of Villa's outlaw band, Pershing's men had been unable to find either Villa or any of his top subordinates.

On May 4, 1916, Pershing ordered Patton to take three automobiles and some men and go to nearby ranches and purchase corn for the army's pack animals. Patton and his convoy, which included himself, ten soldiers, two civilian guides and two civilian chauffeurs, drove off. After they had made their purchases, Patton's force came upon a band of 50 to 60 unarmed but suspicious looking Mexicans in the town of Rubio. Patton later wrote that the men appeared to be "a bad lot. One of my guides [E. L.] Holmdahl, an ex-Villa soldier, recognized a number of old friends among them."

Patton knew that one of Villa's top subordinates, General Julio Cárdenas, had a ranchero at San Miguelito about ten miles north of Rubio. Thinking that Cárdenas might be at the ranchero, Patton outlined a plan to his men—a surprise attack in which the three automobiles would speed into the ranchero, surround the hacienda, trap everyone inside and, hopefully, capture Cárdenas.

The attack was launched at, to use the Old West phrase, "high noon." The three troop-laden cars roared into the quiet ranchero and quickly surrounded the hacienda. Patton's car screeched to a halt on the northwest side of the house, and the other two cars lurched to a stop on the southwest side. Patton jumped out and ran around to the big arched door leading into the patio.

As he did so, on the other side of the hacienda, three armed men on horses attempted to escape south, but found themselves galloping toward the two-car force of Patton's men. Quickly they reversed themselves and headed north—straight for Patton. All three mounted men fired at the lone American army officer who stood between them and freedom. Patton ordered them to halt, and when they refused, fired his pistol at them until it was empty.

Patton dove for cover around an adobe wall, unsure if he had hit any of the men. The situation became chaotic as gunfire erupted from all around. Holmdahl and two other men managed to reach Patton as he was reloading. During a lull in the shooting, Patton scampered up onto the roof of the hacienda to see if he could spot any other bandits. As he was walking along the roof, it suddenly gave way beneath him. The next thing Patton knew, he had plunged through the roof up to his armpits, his lower body dangling helplessly in the room below. Patton desperately pulled himself back onto the roof before anyone inside could attack him. By this time all shooting had stopped. From his vantage point Patton could not see any bandits. A search inside the hacienda revealed only frightened women and children.

After their search of the ranchero was complete, Patton and his men discovered that their attack was a success. Three bandits, including General Cárdenas, were dead. No one in his command suffered any injury. Patton ordered the three bodies loaded onto the cars. His convoy drove off just as a rescue force of 50 mounted bandits rode into sight. Patton and his men escaped just in time.

News of Patton's adventure and its success briefly turned him into a national hero. Newspapers, hungry for any good news about the Punitive Expedition, lauded him

General George S. Patton, Jr. (U.S. Army)

Patton had a high-pitched voice which was startling the first time people heard it, because it was such a contrast to his martial reputation.

Lieutenant George Patton at camp during the Punitive Expedition.
(National Archives)

General John Pershing, second from left, Francisco "Pancho" Villa, center, and General Álvaro Obregón. This photograph, taken in 1914. Three years later Patton would participate in the futile attempt to capture the man who was once within arm's reach of Pershing. (National Archives)

A supply train for the Punitive Expedtion. (U.S. Army)

as the "Bandit Killer." By February 1917, the Punitive Expedition concluded with Pershing's troops returning to the United States. Patton's raid was a minor, though sensational, incident in a campaign that failed to achieve its goal. Even so, Patton's initiative had caused the raid to become a landmark in the history of warfare. For the first time ever, a unit of the U.S. Army had launched an attack using motorized transport. Patton had ushered in the age of motorized warfare.

CAMPAIGN: In the military, a series of attacks designed to defeat enemy forces and ultimately cause the enemy to surrender.

DWIGHT D. EISENHOWER *A Captain in Rank, a Colonel in Responsibility*

Biography in Brief

DWIGHT DAVID "IKE" EISEN-HOWER (1890-1960) graduated from West Point in 1915. He participated in World War I (1914-1918) and World War II (1939-1945). During World War I he remained in the United States as a trainer of troops. His career skyrocketed in World War II. In September 1941, he was promoted to brigadier general, in March 1942, to major general, in July 1942, to lieutenant general, in February 1943, to general, and on December 20, 1944, to General of the Army.

He commanded Allied forces in North Africa and Europe, and was responsible for some of the most complex military campaigns in history, including D-Day, the invasion of France on June 6, 1944. As Supreme Headquarters Allied Expeditionary Force (SHAEF), he led the Allies to victory over Nazi Germany in May 1945. He became Army Chief of Staff on November 19, 1945. In 1950, President Harry S Truman appointed him the first Supreme Allied Commander Europe (SACEUR), commander of North Atlantic Treaty Organization (NATO) forces. In 1952 Eisenhower became the Republican party presidential candidate, defeating Douglas Mac-Arthur. Eisenhower went on to win the presidential election of 1952. He served two terms, then retired to his home in Gettysburg, Pennsylvania. He died at the Walter Reed Army Medical Center in 1969.

This account is of his service in World War I and the extraordinary challenges he confronted.

The United States entered World War I in 1917 on the side of the Allies led by Great Britain, France, and Italy against the Central Powers of Germany, Austria-Hungary, and the Ottoman Empire. Although the war had been waged since 1914, the United States was militarily unprepared when Congress declared war. The U.S. Army had only about 110,000 men and ranked seventeenth in the world. In addition to the small army, the United States had a small navy and almost no air force. Literally overnight that changed. The day following the declaration of war, hundreds of thousands of men began enlisting in the services, and orders were placed for everything from shoes to shells, tents to tanks, and ships to airplanes.

The sudden call-up of men placed an incredible strain on the military. Like the other armed services, the U.S. Army abruptly found itself short of everything needed to wage war—except men. Despite the handicap of shortages of uniforms, rifles, helmets, tents and bedding, transportation—even training camps—the spirit of "can do" and "make do" united the professional soldiers with the new conscripts and volunteers in a common cause to teach and learn the art of soldiering in order to wage war in the trenches of France.

Captain Dwight Eisenhower was caught up in the middle of all the frenetic activity. Like his fellow officers, he had been closely following the progress of the war in Europe since its outbreak in 1914. Although the United States had fought in the recent conflicts of the Spanish-American War and the Philippine Insurrection as well as the two expeditions into Mexico, these were skirmishes barely worth mentioning when compared to the great campaigns going on in France. The last true war fought by the United States was the Civil War, more than 50 years earlier. So it was with great anticipation that professional officers, such as Eisenhower, greeted the news of America's entry on the side of the Allies with enthusiasm. At last they would have the opportunity to put to the test their education and training and prove themselves worthy of the uniform they wore.

By March 1918, officers including Major General John J. Pershing, Colonel Douglas MacArthur, Major George C. Marshall, and Lt. Colonel George S. Patton, Jr., were in France. Pershing was the commander of the American Expeditionary Force, a force that would ultimately contain more than two million men. MacArthur was commander of the 42nd "Rainbow" Division, Marshall was a staff officer, and Patton was the first commander of the army's first tank unit. But Eisenhower was not in that group in France. Although he had only been in the army two years, he had already established a reputation as an excellent trainer of men. In fact, to his regret, he was too good at the job. As a result, instead of remaining with the units he trained and leading them to action in France, he found himself repeatedly reassigned to new units for training. Despite his every effort to get himself transferred to France, the War Department kept him in the States. The War Department had plenty of men ready and willing to fight. The critical shortage was in officers capable of training men to be soldiers and teaching them how to fight.

In mid-March 1918, it finally appeared that Eisenhower's luck had changed. He had impressed his superiors in the way he had efficiently assisted in the organization, training, and equipping of the 301st Tank Battalion. He learned that his reward was that he would accompany the unit when it shipped to France—as its commander! Eisenhower's joy lasted two days. Forty-eight hours later new orders came in. Instead of leading men into battle, he would once again be training men for someone else to lead, this time at a place called Camp Colt, located on one of the most hallowed locations in American military history, Gettysburg. Eisenhower buried his disappointment in work, determined to "soldier on" and do his duty.

Duty at Camp Colt would present him with challenges greater than any he had previously faced. He assumed command of Camp Colt on March 24, 1918, where he was made responsible for the stateside training of men in the army's Tank Corps—the first of its kind. Some of those men would ultimately serve in Patton's unit. Eisenhower had to report twice

A photograph of Cadet Dwight Eisenhower that appeared in the 1915 edition of the West Point yearbook, Howitzer. (West Point Museum)

CORPS: A specialized branch or department of the military establishment. Also may refer to a tactical unit usually consisting of two or more divisions.

REQUISITION: In the military, a formal demand for something needed.

a week to Colonel Ira C. Welborn, his commanding officer based in Washington, D.C. Aside from that, he observed, "I was very much on my own at Camp Colt." Captain Eisenhower had less than three years experience as an officer in the army. The task for someone so new to command was enormous. "The Tank Corps was new," he later wrote. "There were no precedents except in basic training, and I was the only regular officer in command. Now I really began to learn about responsibility."

His orders were precise. He was "required to take in volunteers, equip, organize, and instruct them and have them ready for overseas shipment when called upon." The orders also warned him that "no excuses for deficiencies in their records or equipment would be accepted." The consequences could not be more stark and draconian. Captain Eisenhower would have to successfully train all his men, or he would be relieved of command and his career would be finished.

Camp Colt was designed to accommodate four thousand men, but it still lacked many basic amenities. Five hundred men were stationed at Camp Colt in early April 1918 when a violent snowstorm struck. None of the tents had stoves. Eisenhower promptly decided to requisition stoves from the hardware stores in Gettysburg. The trip from Camp Colt to

Eisenhower (middle row, third from left) and members of the West Point football team. The team included two other future generals that achieved fame in World War II: James Van Fleet (back row, far left) and Omar Bradley (back row, fourth from left). (West Point Museum)

the town normally took two minutes. That day, the trip took two hours. Even though he obtained every stove that would fit into a tent, he discovered that he was still short of heating units. Fortunately, the land in and around Gettysburg is very rocky. Boulders and shards of shale that had been trod upon by troops in blue and gray in July 1863 were, under Eisenhower's orders, gathered to form stone cairns for the fires that would warm khaki-clad soldiers in April 1918. Having an open flame inside a tent is dangerous, and as a safety precaution, Eisenhower organized a patrol of men to keep watch during the night, making sure that the fires were properly stoked and that no tent burned down.

As the weather warmed and more men arrived at the camp, Eisenhower confronted yet another challenge as a result of insufficient supplies. His orders were to train men to be tankers, but he had no tanks. He wasn't sure when—or if—he would ever receive any. In order to keep his men usefully occupied, he asked for suggestions from his junior officers. The result was an outpouring of ideas. One suggestion concerned the need for clear and accurate communication between frontline units and headquarters. "We realized that anyone who could learn telegraphy and master Morse code would be useful in the Tank Corps," Eisenhower later recalled. Classes were immediately organized. Another suggestion resulted in the creation of a motor school using any second-hand engine they could find for training in engine maintenance and repair.

Eisenhower went to Washington, D.C., to obtain cannons and received some obsolete small cannons from the navy. Men were trained in the operation of the cannons, even though they were not designed for tanks and there was no ammunition. When some machine guns arrived, one of the men suggested that they be mounted on truck trailers or the flatbeds of trucks so the men could learn how to fire the weapons from mobile platforms. "The only satisfactory place for firing was Big Round Top," Eisenhower recalled. "Its base made a perfect backstop. Soon soldiers were shooting from moving trucks at all kinds of targets there and the firing might have been heavier than during [the Battle of Gettysburg]."

Men kept arriving, forcing Eisenhower to expand the size of

Eisenhower standing in front of a World War I Renault tank. Eisenhower used tanks like this for training at Camp Colt. (Official U.S. Army photograph, Dwight D. Eisenhower Library)

MORSE CODE: A method of communication in which letters of the alphabet and numbers are represented by dots and dashes or long and short signals.

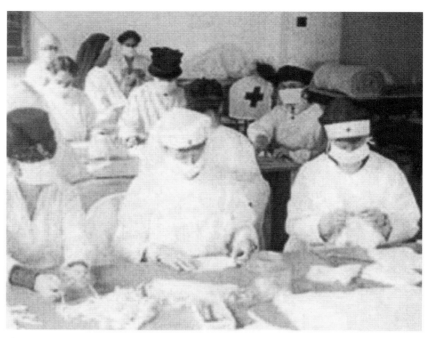

Gauze surgical masks became popular items during the influenza pandemic because it was believed that they helped prevent the spread of the disease. Here nurses wearing gauze masks are preparing masks for distribution. (Library of Congress)

TACTICS: In the military, the method used to overwhelm an enemy.

the camp. By mid-July, he was supervising the training of 10,000 men and 600 officers. It was also during the summer that three small French-manufactured Renault tanks arrived. The tanks, which weighed seven tons—or 14,000 pounds—each were designed to carry either a small cannon or a machine gun. The three arrived without any weapons. "Again, we improvised," Eisenhower later wrote. .

As summer turned into fall, Eisenhower confronted a problem that was sweeping the world, an epidemic known as "Spanish flu." It was a virulent, swiftly spreading disease that would become the worst epidemic of the twentieth century. Approximately 25 percent of the world's population caught the disease. Approximately 28 percent, or more than 26 million people, in the United States were stricken. The first case was reported in Massachusetts on September 8, 1918.

On September 14, 1918, the first cases were diagnosed at Camp Colt. Eisenhower, and the camp's chief surgeon, Lieutenant Colonel Thomas Scott, promptly used a variety of precautions to contain the spread of the disease, including the isolation of anyone showing symptoms. Those who fell sick were given a number of treatments, but in truth there was little the doctors could do except let the disease run its course.

For 150 men, unfortunately, the disease proved fatal. As men died, they were taken to a separate tent where they would be processed for burial. In one case, the medical attendants were overzealous in their removal. As Eisenhower later recalled, "One man, who had been very sick and had apparently stopped breathing, had been carried out of the hospital by orderlies and put inside the morgue tent." Troops were filing past the tent when, hours later the man awoke. "Completely bewildered by his surroundings, and alarmed when he saw that he was surrounded by [dead] bodies, he called out in a weak and weird voice, 'Get me out of here.'" But instead of bringing assistance, his cry so thoroughly frightened the men on the other side of the tent wall who heard him that they started a stampede. Eventually one soldier calmed down enough to tell the doctors what had happened, and the poor enlisted man was rescued from the morgue.

Colonel Wellborn, had been very impressed with Eisenhower's performance at Camp Colt and in recognition,

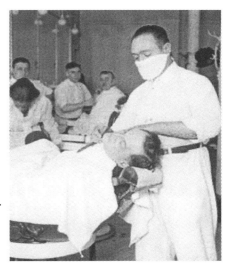

Even simple things such as getting a haircut became a challenge during the influenza pandemic. Note, however, that the people in the background are not wearing surgical masks. (Library of Congress)

This is perhaps the most famous photograph of Eisenhower taken during World War II. He is talking to a member of the 101st Airborne prior to D-Day on June 6, 1944. In the weeks leading up to Operation Overlord, the invasion of Normandy, Eisenhower visited as many of the American units involved in the invasion. (National Archives)

A 1990 postage stamp commemorating the centennial of Eisenhower's birth. In the background of the stamp is a reproduction of a scene of Eisenhower talking to paratroopers prior to the D-Day landing in World War II. (Author's collection)

he recommended that Eisenhower be promoted to major. In his report he stated in part, "While Captain Eisenhower is a junior captain and is not eligible for promotion, according to the policy of the War Department, it is urgently requested that an exception be made in his case. He is doing important work, is deserving of promotion, and his duties can be better performed with the increased rank." On July 22, 1918, Eisenhower was promoted to major. Then on October 14, 1918, at the age of 28, he was promoted to lieutenant colonel. In seven months, he had advanced two grades. Although he did not go to the war in Europe, he at least had the satisfaction of knowing that he had succeeded in the "training war" in the United States.

Dwight Eisenhower was one of six boys in his family. All the sons had to share in the family chores. One chore was washing the laundry. At the turn of the twentieth century, clothes were not washed by automated machines. It was a complicated and laborious process done by hand and with boiling water. Disposable diapers also did not exist back then, and Dwight and his older brothers learned very quickly that the worst part of laundry was washing the soiled cloth diapers of their baby brothers.

MAURICE ROSE *A Teenage Boy Leads Men to War*

Maurice Rose was only 17 years old when the United States entered World War I in April 1917. Being below the minimum enlistment age of 18 years did not stop him. Caught up in the patriotic spirit that swept the nation, he wanted to join the army and help in the fight to, in President Woodrow Wilson's words, "make the world safe for democracy." Even though his father was a rabbi and there was no military tradition in the family, young Rose convinced his parents to grant their permission for him to enlist. He became one of the first men in his hometown of Denver, Colorado, to do so. Shortly after his induction, he applied for an officer's training program and, after passing the entrance examinations in which he scored near the top of the list, he was accepted. On August 11, 1917, three months before he would reach his eighteenth birthday, Maurice Rose was commissioned a second lieutenant in the U.S. Army. Four months later, at age eighteen, he was promoted to first lieutenant. He was too young to vote; in those days the minimum voting age was twenty-one. But very soon he would lead men his age and older into battle.

Training in drills, the command of men, and other aspects of army life continued at a frenetic pace until, on June 1, 1918, Rose, now a part of the 353rd Infantry Regiment, left the United States aboard the British ship HMS *Karmala* for Liverpool, England. He and his unit then boarded another ship, and on June 22, he arrived in France. Immediately Rose and his men were given additional training to prepare them for the kind of fighting they would encounter. Sometime in early September he learned that his unit would participate in the upcoming St. Mihiel Offensive.

Although individual American units had assisted their British and French allies in earlier battles, the St. Mihiel Offensive was the first large-scale campaign conducted by the American Expeditionary Force. Scheduled to start on September 12, 1918, the five-day operation would include nine American and four French divisions all under the command of the leader of the American Expeditionary Force,

Biography in Brief
MAURICE ROSE (1899-1945) was 17 years old when he was commissioned a second lieutenant on August 11, 1917. He served in World War I (1914-1918) and World War II (1939-1945). In 1930 he transferred from the infantry to the cavalry and in 1940 to the newly established Armored Force. In early 1942, he served as the chief of staff to Major General George Patton.

During World War II he fought in North Africa, Sicily, France, and Germany. In 1943 Rose, a colonel, was promoted to brigadier general, and in 1944, to major general. As the commander of the 3rd Armored "Spearhead" Division, he led the American First Army advance through France into Germany.

On March 30, 1945, while with forward units in Germany, he was captured by a German panzer detachment, and in the process of surrendering, he was killed by enemy fire. Rose was the highest ranking Jewish-American soldier killed in action during World War II.

The following event occurred in World War I.

DRILL: Disciplined, repetitious exercise and training designed to teach a skill.

Major General Maurice Rose.
(AP/Wide World)

General John J. Pershing. The attack would be against nine well-entrenched German divisions in and around the occupied French city of St. Mihiel.

After three brutal years of war in which millions of their soldiers had been killed, the war-weary British and French were publicly glad to have reinforcements of fresh American divisions. At the same time, their military and political leaders were privately concerned about how well the Americans would perform on the battlefield against an experienced German army considered the best in the world. The United States had no military tradition comparable to the Europeans. In fact, there were only about 110,000 men in the army when the United States declared war. Yet, in one breathtaking year, the

United States had inducted, trained, and shipped approximately two million soldiers to France. The administrative and organizational success in creating such a large military force in so short of a time had gained the Europeans' respect. But would these hastily trained soldiers, so recently removed from the civilian world, fight? Would their equally hastily trained sergeants and officers be able to successfully lead them into battle? For good or ill, the St. Mihiel Offensive would answer that question.

The city of St. Mihiel is located in the eastern French province of Lorraine on the Meuse River. The German army had captured the city in 1914 and had successfully held it ever since. St. Mihiel was the tip of a long German salient into French territory. Holding St. Mihiel allowed the Germans to threaten Allied communication and railroad lines running parallel along the southern border of the salient. If the American offensive succeeded, it would prove American troops' battleworthiness. It would also, according to General Pershing free "the Paris-Nancy rail communications and the roads that paralleled the Meuse north from St. Mihiel [and make them] available for our use in the greater offensive," meaning the larger Meuse-Argonne Offensive scheduled to start on September 26.

Lieutenant Rose's unit was a part of the 89th Division positioned north of the French village of Flirey and facing the forest Bois de Mort Mare. Their mission was to push north through the forest and past the village of Thiaucourt approximately five miles away. Entrenched between the forest and Thiaucourt were row upon row of heavily defended German trenches and machine gun nests. Rejecting the methodical, frontal assaults used by the French and British generals, which had resulted in horrendous casualties and little gain, General Pershing had his men trained in fast-moving flanking attacks designed, wherever possible, to strike at enemy positions from the side.

At 1:00 A.M.—0100—on September 12, 1918, a four-hour American artillery barrage designed to cripple the enemy front line troops and reinforcements began. Then at 5:00 A.M., came the signal to attack, four loud blasts of the company com-

Map of Europe at the start of World War I. (Author's collection)

SALIENT: In the military, a fortified projection into enemy territory.

American troops at a section of the Argonne Forest. Note the battle-scarred trees in the background.
(Courtesy U.S. Army Signal Corps)

The Army tells time in hours numbered from one to twenty-four. For example, one o'clock in the morning is 0100 hours, noon is 1200 hours, 4:30 in the afternoon is 1630 hours, and midnight is 2400 hours.

manders' whistles, was heard. Rose then lifted his arm high over his head, motioned to his men, and shouted, "Follow me!" With his Colt .45 automatic in hand, he clambered up the steep slope of the trench and went "over the top." With his men close behind, they charged through the desolate no man's land, the battle-scarred territory that lay between the two armies, and attacked the German positions.

Rose's biographers, Steven L. Ossad and Don R. Marsh, described what happened next. "The enemy's 77-mm guns and trench mortars exploded among the advancing men with high explosives, and as they crossed the ground in front of the enemy trenches, the deadly rattle of machine guns and sharp cracking sound of rifle fire could be heard over the shell explosions. Rose maintained the line of advance, leading his doughboys forward even as men fell around him or disappeared in the explosions. As they reached the trenches and infiltrated them from the rear, there was heavy hand-to-hand fighting, and large numbers of prisoners and machine guns were captured. Pershing's emphasis on 'open warfare,' the aggressive use of rifle and bayonet, was paying off."

With the coming of the night, the advance paused, and the Americans consolidated the day's gains and brought up fresh supplies and reinforcements for the next day's advance. The Germans fiercely resisted the American attack on September 13, using artillery mortars with deadly efficiency against the charging troops, causing many casualties. One of those casualties was Lieutenant Rose who was wounded by shrapnel. He also suffered a concussion when an enemy shell exploded near him.

When stretcher-bearers tried to carry him back to the first aid stations in the rear, Rose ordered them away to take back the more seriously wounded soldiers first. Rose continued to lead his men. Eventually, weakened by loss of blood, he collapsed and was carried back. At the aid station the doctors and medics quickly dressed his wounds and had him shipped to the division's base hospital located at Flirey.

The doctors had told him his wounds would keep him out of action for months, Rose defied the doctors and left the hospital without authorization. He returned to his unit in time to participate in the latter part of the Meuse-Argonne Offensive.

The impact of the American success in the St. Mihiel Offensive was enormous. As General Pershing later wrote, "The St. Mihiel victory probably did more than any single operation of the war to encourage the tired Allies. After the years of doubt and despair, of suffering and loss, it brought them assurance of the final defeat of an enemy whose armies had seemed well-nigh invincible."

Acclaim for the American army's success was quickly forthcoming. Field Marshal Ferdinand Foch, supreme commander of the Allied forces, wrote to Pershing, stating, "The American First Army . . . has won a magnificent victory by a maneuver as skillfully prepared as it was valiantly executed." It was a sentiment echoed by Field Marshal Sir Douglas Haig, commander of the British troops in France, who wrote, "All ranks of the British Armies in France welcome with unbounded admiration and pleasure the victory which has attended the initial offensive of the great American army . . . ."

For Maurice Rose, the American success on the battlefield had a profound personal meaning. While convalescing in the hospital, he had the opportunity to reflect on the recent events of his life and what he wished to do in the future. Most men wounded in action would have been happy to complete their service, accept an honorable discharge, and then return to

American soldiers bringing loaves of bread to the troops. A rope was strung through the middle of the loaves allowing for easy transport. (U.S. Army Signal Corps)

CASUALTY: A person who is killed, wounded, captured, or missing in military action.

DOUGHBOY: The nick-name for American infantry-men from about 1867 to 1918. Several theories exist as to the word's origin. One of them is that the uniform's large brass buttons resembled a pastry called doughboy.

civilian life. But Rose had displayed a talent for leadership and had discovered that he loved military life and wanted to remain and advance in the career. Anti-Semitism and anti-Catholicism, however, were widespread in the army at that time. Rose knew that for someone of the Jewish faith, a military career with advancement would be all but impossible. On September 26, 1918, while still in the hospital and during a routine inquiry for medical records, as Ossad and Marsh later wrote, 18-year-old "Maurice Rose declared to Captain D. A. Thom of the Medical Corps that he was a Protestant." Rose never told anyone why he did this, and he never left any written record of explanation. On a personal level he continued to observe Jewish customs with his family and loved ones, but as of September 26, 1918, according to the U.S. Army, he was officially a Protestant.

An American troop convoy. Note that in addition to trucks, the convoy also has horse drawn wagons. (U.S. Army Signal Corps)

LEWIS B. "CHESTY" PULLER *The Legend of El Tigre*

In 1919, Marine lieutenant Lewis "Chesty" Puller was an unhappy 20-year-old man. World War I had ended in 1918 before he could participate. Thanks to the postwar demobilization that drastically reduced the military ranks, he had been discharged. The only way he could remain in the Marine Corps that he had come to love was if he reentered as an enlisted man. He did not hesitate and was made a corporal. When he heard that the Haitian government had requested help from the U.S. government to put down Caco insurrectionists, Puller volunteered to be a part of the Marine force that would help restore law and order to that country.

When he arrived in Haiti later that year, he was made an acting first lieutenant in the Haitian gendarmerie, or police force. His first assignment was to take pack trains of mules loaded with supplies to isolated outposts in the Caco-controlled interior. His ability to do so, and repel Caco attempts to stop him, impressed his superiors. Soon he was given command of a company of about one hundred Haitians and orders to clear out the Caco bandits that were marauding the Mirebalais-Loscahobas region in central Haiti.

Puller's unit was a colorful and largely untrained band. The most notable among the group was his top subordinate officer, Lieutenant Napoleon Lyautey. A dignified and aristocratic individual who possessed large portions of knowledge, wisdom, and common sense, Lyautey had earlier been a marshal in the army of one of Haiti's previous governments. Another memorable soldier was Corporal Cermontoute, a headhunter who proudly exhibited his trophies to his new commanding officer during their first meeting. In addition, Puller discovered that his command included over a hundred native women—camp followers who did the cooking, laundry, and other domestic duties.

Puller had only two days of training before he was to take his company into the jungle. He plunged into the task. Almost from the moment he put on a Marine Corps uniform, Puller displayed an outstanding ability to train even the rawest of

Biography in Brief
LEWIS BURWELL "CHESTY" PULLER (1898-1971) fought in the Banana Wars (1914-1933), World War II (1939-1945), and the Korean War (1950-1953).

Puller fought in battles both great and obscure, beginning in Haiti and Nicaragua during the Banana Wars. In World War II he fought on Guadalcanal, Cape Gloucester, and Peleliu. During the Korean War, he participated in the landing at Inchon and the withdrawal from the Changjin Reservoir.

Puller became a brigadier general in January 1951. In 1953, he was promoted to major general, and on October 30, 1955, the day of his retirement from the Marine Corps, he was promoted to lieutenant general. He set countless examples of extraordinary heroism and selfless leadership, and along the way, earned 53 decorations. He became the only man awarded a total of five Navy Crosses—a decoration of valor second only to the Medal of Honor.

His most famous nickname was "Chesty," given for a voice that could carry like a bullhorn. Before that he had another nickname, one earned in Haiti at the beginning of his career. Herewith is presented an early episode in the legend of El Tigre—the Tiger.

> MARKSMANSHIP: Training designed to develop skill and accuracy in shooting.

Lieutenant General Lewis "Chesty" Puller. (USMC)

recruits. He developed a compressed program that focused on marksmanship and drill fundamentals using a bugler since, in the thick Haitian jungle, his men would not be able to see hand signs. Additionally, to bolster confidence and increase the impact of his unit's firepower, he reorganized his squads into four-man fire teams—something that no one had ever done before. A fire team working closely together would both increase the confidence of the individual members and the effectiveness of its shooting.

Two days later, as ordered, the training period was over. Puller led his motley group into the Caco-controlled jungle. At first Puller made his patrols by the rule book, conducting searches during the day and camping down at night. The result was that he and his force spent one futile day after another vainly searching for bandits. Finally Lt. Lyautey and another subordinate officer, Lt. Brunot, approached Puller and made a suggestion. "We are wasting time with so much daylight marching," they said. "We must move by night if we wish to catch the Cacos in camp." Puller liked the idea. From that moment on, his company would camp during the daylight hours in an easily defensible location and do its searching for bandits at night.

On the second night using this new tactic, Puller, leading a small patrol, saw in the distance a cluster of campfires on a nearby ridge. His men confirmed his suspicion: ahead was what appeared to be a major Caco camp. In order to be able to quietly scout the site, Puller took off his combat boots and replaced them with a pair of old basketball sneakers that he carried for this purpose. Three other men, who would accompany him, simply took off their boots and went barefoot. Led by Puller, they quietly approached the camp and conducted a reconnaissance. Puller's impression was confirmed. They had indeed found a major Caco sanctuary. Puller estimated that it contained more than one hundred men who were engaged in a noisy celebration and, Puller was happy to note, oblivious to the thought that their supposedly safe location would soon be attacked. In a few hours, most, if not all, of the celebrants would fall into an exhausted sleep. Though he had not been in Haiti for a very long time, Puller had already learned a lot about the Caco way of fighting. Even though the Cacos here had more men than he did, if Puller could

Puller when he was a second lieutenant. (National Archives)

Puller, center, in Nicaragua.
(USMC Historical Center)

A Caco prisoner, center, escorted by two Marines. (National Archives)

launch a surprise attack, the odds were very good that he and his men could defeat them.

Puller and his scouts carefully made their way back to the patrol and then quietly regrouped with the rest of the company. Puller promptly outlined the trap he planned to spring at dawn on the Cacos. Fully aware of his men's lack of training, Puller made sure his plan was simple. Once he was confident his men understood what they had to do, he began leading them into position. First he positioned most of the company in an assault line along one side of the ridge facing the camp. He then took his machine gun crews just past the camp and off to the left where he positioned them so that they had a clear field of fire on the route Puller gambled that the Cacos would take once they started to retreat. With a confident tone meant to inspire his men, he said, "[The Cacos] will run after the first firing, and they'll run right into our field of fire."

The Caco celebration had almost completely ended, and most of the Cacos were asleep when, precisely at dawn, Puller led his assault line in the attack. As he had hoped, the surprise was complete. His men's opening rifle volley stunned the bandits who put up almost no resistance. Instead, panic-stricken, they rushed pell-mell away from the attack—and precisely down the retreat path covered by Puller's machine gun crews.

The victory was spectacular for the lightly trained force. After the fighting had stopped, Puller counted seventeen enemy dead. He could only guess at how many were wounded. In comparison, none of his men were even scratched. Puller's men and the camp followers excitedly occupied the Caco sanctuary and proceeded to collect the booty that included rifles, ammunition, and other supplies—and a crowing flock of more than two hundred gamecocks. Gamecocks were highly prized in Haiti. A find of this size made their victory truly a glorious event. As Puller stood by and watched, cook fires were started, pots were filled with water and rice, and a cockfight tournament celebrating their victory commenced. For the rest of the day, Puller's men watched cockfights and feasted off

88

A Marine patrol in Haiti, 1919. Note the use of mules to carry supplies. (National Archives)

the defeated roosters whose plucked, dressed, and dismembered carcasses were thrown into the pots with boiling rice.

Puller would later go on to fight guerillas in Nicaragua as well. Before his tour of fighting in the Banana Wars was over, friend and foe would call him El Tigre—"the Tiger."

Puller's family had deep roots in American history. One of Puller's distant relatives was the patriot Patrick Henry. A number of Puller's ancestors fourght for the Confederacy in the Civil War. Puller was also a distant cousin of George S. Patton, Jr.

ELWOOD "PETE" QUESADA *The Mail Must Get Through*

Biography in Brief

ELWOOD RICHARD "PETE" QUESADA (1904-1993) Quesada was a Hispanic-American general who was an innovative pioneer in tactical air-ground operations. Quesada received his lieutenant's commission in the Army Air Corps (then a part of the Army) in April 1927. In the years between World War I and World War II he flew every airplane in the Air Corps inventory, becoming one of the most experienced pilots in the service.

On December 11, 1942, by order of Army Chief of Staff General George Marshall, Major Quesada was promoted directly to brigadier general. On April 28, 1944, he was promoted to major general. As the commanding general of the 9th Tactical Air Command in Europe during World War II, Quesada successfully developed the tactics of forward air control in combined air-ground operations that aided the rapid Allied advance through France.

In October 1947, he was promoted to lieutenant general. He retired from the Air Force in October 1951. In 1958, he became the first director of the Federal Aviation Administration under President Dwight Eisenhower.

The following account occurred in 1934, when President Franklin Roosevelt revoked all the civilian airline airmail contracts and tasked the Air Corps to take over the routes. First Lieutenant "Pete" Quesada was one of the pilots assigned to deliver the mail.

The airmail system in the United States of the early 1930s was composed of 34 mail routes that covered 27,000 miles of airways. These routes were assigned to private commercial airline companies by the Post Office in a process called the negotiated contract. Suspicions of excess profits and corruption had surrounded the process for years. Alabama Senator Hugo Black had been investigating the process for some time. On January 26, 1934, he told President Franklin Roosevelt, "the whole system of airmail contracts . . . was fraudulent and completely illegal."

The Great Depression was at its height. The airmail contract situation was seen as a scandal that involved corporations making excess profits while millions of people were out of work and struggling to survive. President Roosevelt was anxious to act, but if he canceled the airmail contracts, he needed to be able to have a substitute system ready to use.

On the morning of February 9, 1934, Major General Benjamin Foulois, the commander of the Army Air Corps, met with Second Assistant Postmaster General Harllee Branch who asked him, "If the President should cancel the contracts, do you think the Air Corps could carry the mail to keep the system operating?"

"Yes, sir," Foulois answered. "If you want us to carry the mail, we'll do it."

Because no official announcement had yet been made, Foulois, after he returned to his office, ordered his staff to quietly develop a plan for the Air Corps to take over airmail service. Then, that afternoon Army Chief of Staff General Douglas MacArthur met Foulois and said, "A newsman has just told me that the President has released an Executive Order giving the Air Corps the job of flying the mail. . . . The question is, can you do it?" Foulois told MacArthur that, with the proper support, the Air Corps could. MacArthur nodded and said, "Yell when you need help from me and keep me informed. It's your ball game."

The Curtis Condor. (Courtesy U.S. Army)

The Air Corps had just ten days to prepare. The task was enormous. Short of time, short of money, short of proper equipment, short of experience, and under the national spotlight, nonetheless the men in the Air Corps from General Foulois down to the lowest airplane mechanic were eager to take on the challenge. They knew that the stakes of the effort extended beyond the delivery of the mail. The *New York Times* reported, "The cancellation of airmail contracts will probably have a far-reaching effect upon the development of commercial and military air service. The proponents of a separate Air Force . . . see for the first time an opportunity to obtain their objective."

Despite the scandal of excess profit-taking by the airline companies, Roosevelt's decision was controversial. Many companies, not just the airlines, as well as Roosevelt's political opponents were vocal in their belief that the Air Corps would fail. Lieutenant Colonel Henry H. "Hap" Arnold acknowledged this when he wrote, ". . . They are waiting like hungry dogs to grab up any mistake or misfortune which may overtake us and make the most of it."

It was against this backdrop of political drama that Lieutenant Elwood "Pete" Quesada found himself. With more than 3,000 hours of flying time in a wide variety of planes and under every weather condition, Quesada was one of the ten most experienced pilots in the Air Corps. Assigned Section Chief on the Newark, New Jersey/Cleveland, Ohio route, he was well aware of how great the challenge was. Quesada knew

Quesada got the nickname, "Pete" from a fellow Air Corps recruit in the 1920s when, after he had introduced himself using his full name, Elwood Richard Quesada, one of the recruits replied, "Forget that. You're Pete!"

Captain Ross Hoyt, pilot of the refueling plane, far left, and the crew of the airplane named Question Mark, *from left to right, Captain Ira Eaker, Major General James Fechet, Major Carl Spaatz, Lieutenant Elwood Quesada, and Master Sergeant Roy Hooe. In January 1929, the* Question Mark *set the endurance record for continuous flight, staying aloft 150 hours and 40 minutes. This was made possible by a primitive aerial refueling process from Captain Hoyt's plane to the* Question Mark. (USAF)

that flying the mail routes was dangerous. Radar had not yet been invented, there were very few night-flying instruments in the cockpit, and primitive radio beacons for guidance were still being installed across the country. Just a few months earlier, one of the major airlines had lost eleven pilots and crew in accidents. Shortly after the Air Corps took control of the airmail routes, three pilots were killed in accidents.

Quesada, however, was not intimidated. He knew his plane, the twin-engined Condor B-2 biplane. Although it had recently been classified as obsolete, it had many of the features needed for flying the airmail route. It was reliable, had a range of almost a thousand miles, and unlike many planes in the Air Corps inventory, it had an enclosed cockpit, modern instrumentation, and a radio that could pick up all the communications frequencies. Also, Quesada's crew chief who flew with him on the routes was Master Sergeant Roy Hooe. Hooe knew airplanes inside and out and could fix anything.

Quesada's schedule called for him to depart Newark at 11:00 P.M. They would make one scheduled refueling stop at Bellefonte, Pennsylvania, and then continue to Cleveland. Warm in the comfort of the enclosed cockpit, Quesada, with earphones in place, listened to the steady radio signal that guided him along his route. Timing was everything, for the navigation beams overlapped each other at preset locations. If a pilot drifted off course, the beam would fade. If the pilot got so off course that he lost the beam, the pilot would lose precious time, and fuel spent in regaining the signal. If too much time was lost, the pilot would find himself running out of fuel before reaching the airstrip. Since there were very few airports in the country at the time, the pilot would have to land in an open field or on a road, but for Quesada, keeping centered on the beam was almost routine.

One night, when they landed to refuel at Bellefonte, it was 20 degrees below zero. Even though their leather flying suits were wool-lined, Quesada and Hooe immediately felt the cold as they stepped out of the Condor and onto the hard-packed snow, their breath forming clouds of steam in the frigid air. They were the only people on the field, but they knew where the key to the fuel pump was. While Hooe got the key, Quesada climbed up onto the engines and unscrewed the gas caps. The fuel pump at the field was hand-operated, and after they had topped off the gas tanks, the two were numb and aching with cold. Then, after screwing on the gas caps and putting away the pump and equipment, they returned into the Condor to continue the flight. Despite the freezing temperatures, the engines started. With only a wind sock for reference, Quesada took off into the night for Cleveland.

Quesada was able to uphold the Post Office delivery motto of "neither rain, nor snow, nor gloom of night. . . ." But that motto had not encountered the Air Corps bureaucracy. Concern over pilot safety arose after a series of accidents resulted in the death and injuries of a number of pilots. One evening, shortly before Quesada was supposed to take off, he was informed that he could not fly in the Condor because it was classified unsafe. The reason for that was because the only

Lieutenant General Elwood "Pete" Quesada. (USAF)

An early air mail stamp. (Author's collection)

In 1925, Quesada tried out for the St. Louis Cardinals baseball team. Manager Branch Rickey was so impressed with the play of Quesada and one other young ballplayer that he offered them both contracts. Quesada's professional career only lasted a few weeks. The other player was Dizzy Dean, who would go on to became a Hall of Fame pitcher.

exit door in the Condor was in the tail. If there was an emergency, and the pilot had to exit quickly, he had to run down the length of the fuselage in order to escape. The chances of successfully bailing out under such circumstances were considered very slim. When Quesada received the news, he immediately complained to his superior officer, Major B. Q. Jones.

"So, what are you bellyaching about, Pete?" the major asked.

"Major, the B-2's the only plane we've got that you don't have to jump out of!" Quesada replied.

The major asked what Quesada meant.

"It's the only plane we've got in the entire section that's properly instrumented to fly in bad weather. . . . It's got a radio that can receive on almost any frequency. So it's one plane you don't have to worry about. It's just the reverse. It's the other planes that should be grounded!" Quesada answered.

Major Jones thought for a moment, then told Quesada to forget the grounding. Quesada and Hooe got in their Condor and flew off to deliver the mail to Cleveland.

On May 16, 1934, the Air Corps service as airmail courier was concluded. A final report noted that the pilots had flown over one and a half million miles, carried more than 770,000 pounds of mail, completed approximately 75 percent of their flights and, despite accidents, did not lose a single piece of mail. Even though many people thought the Air Corps efforts were a failure, in a final report, Air Corps lieutenant colonel Horace Hickam stated, "No report in Air Mail operations can be complete without commenting on the special efficiency, resourcefulness, fortitude and initiative of Air Corps personnel in all ranks and grades. Adverse weather conditions and inadequate facilities seemed only to spur them to renewed efforts. The manner in which all performed their duties is evidence that the Air Corps can successfully meet any emergency provided the necessary facilities and equipment are available."

VICTOR KRULAK *The Amphibious Boat That Would Help Win a War*

Landing craft design and the tactics of getting men, equipment, and supplies ashore had changed little since the time of the American Revolution. In the decades prior to World War II, visionary leaders in the Marine Corps came to the conclusion that they would have to develop a new doctrine of amphibious assault. But they were repeatedly frustrated because of lack of money and experiments with different boat designs met with repeated failure.

As sometimes happens in history, one man in the right place at the right time discovers the answer to a problem. The man was Lieutenant Victor Krulak, the place was Shanghai, China, located at the mouth of the Yangtse River on the coast of the East China Sea, and the time was 1937 during the invasion of China by the Imperial Japanese Army in the Second Sino-Japanese War. Lt. Krulak was part of a Marine detachment sent to China's largest port to protect Americans living in the city. He learned of a Japanese amphibious assault on Chinese positions nearby in the Liuho area at the mouth of the Yangtse River north and west of Shanghai. Krulak successfully got permission from his superiors and from the Japanese navy to witness the amphibious attack. Sailing in a U.S. Navy tugboat and accompanied by a Navy photographer, Krulak had a ringside seat on the action. Krulak witnessed how Japanese destroyers carried out preliminary bombardment of the beaches, and support fire after the troops had landed. He saw Japanese soldiers debarking from transports and into landing craft. When he saw the landing craft themselves, he excitedly ordered the tug closer and had the photographer take as many pictures as possible. Krulak had seen the answer to the Marines' landing boat problem. As he later wrote, "There we saw, in action, exactly what the Marines had been looking for-sturdy, ramp-bow-type boats capable of transporting heavy vehicles and depositing them directly on the beaches."

When he returned, Krulak wrote his report, taking care to emphasize the wide, square bow, hinged at the base, that per-

Biography in Brief

VICTOR HAROLD "BRUTE" KRULAK (1913-present) fought in World War II (1939-1945), the Korean War (1950-1953), and the Vietnam War (1965-1973). He graduated from the U.S. Naval Academy at Annapolis, Maryland, in 1934 and was commissioned a Marine second lieutenant. In 1937 he was a company commander stationed in Shanghai, China.

In January 1943, Krulak volunteered for parachute training and was among the first "paramarines." In October of that year Krulak, now a lieutenant colonel, commanded the 2nd Parachute Battalion, 1st Marine Amphibious Corps during a diversionary landing on the Pacific island of Choiseul. During that action he earned the Navy Cross and the Purple Heart. At the end of World War II, he helped negotiate the surrender of Japanese forces in the Tsingtao, China area.

In the early part of the Korean War he was the chief of staff of the 1st Marine Division. In July 1956, he was promoted to brigadier general. He was promoted to major general in November 1959. On March 1, 1964, he was promoted to lieutenant general. Krulak retired on May 31, 1968.

This account is from the time when he was a captain in China in 1937. He had an opportunity to observe a Japanese amphibious assault on the port city of Shanghai. It was an opportunity that would have extraordinary consequences.

Marines in a boat called a motor sailer on their way to the beach in a 1924 amphibious landing exercise. (USMC)

Navy corpsmen, in a 1934 exercise, make a typical pre-Higgins boat amphibious landing. (USMC)

mitted the bow to swing open to allow the men to rush out, and the pointed stern of the landing craft. Together with the photographs, the package was sent to Washington. Krulak was convinced that the Navy's Bureau of Ships, which was responsible for shipbuilding, would authorize production of new landing craft based on his report.

But nothing happened.

Two years later, in 1939, Krulak was in Washington and decided to search the files of the Bureau of Ships to see what had happened to his report. When he pulled it out of the cabinet, he discovered that his work had been filed and forgotten—dismissed with the comment written in the margin that it had been composed by "some nut out of China," who obviously couldn't tell a pointed bow from a squared-off stern.

But Krulak refused to allow some faceless bureaucrat to stop him. By this time Japan's war in China had escalated, and even though he could not know that war in Europe would erupt in less than three months, it was obvious to most in the armed services that war in Europe would soon occur. The likelihood of the United States being drawn into a war was only a question of time.

Krulak took his report and a model of a Japanese landing boat he had ordered made and presented them to his Marine superiors, including the Commandant of the Marine Corps Lieutenant General Thomas Holcomb.

ADVOCATE: An individual who speaks in favor of something.

Lieutenant General Victor "Brute" Krulak. (USMC)

General Holcomb came away from the meeting convinced that Krulak's landing boat was just what the Marines needed. Yet, even with the Marine Commandant as an advocate, the Navy resisted.

Meanwhile, at the same time that Krulak was working on his report, a boat builder based in New Orleans by the name of Andrew Higgins had been approached by the Marine Corps to develop landing craft. The design that the Marines felt held the most promise for the transport of

Lieutenant General Holland M. "Howling Mad" Smith (USMC)

men was something called the "Eureka," a powerful shallow draft boat that was used in the bayous of Louisiana.

In March 1941, Krulak was ordered to meet with Higgins, show him his report, photos, and model, and suggest modifications to the Eureka. This time, Krulak met with a receptive and enthusiastic audience. As Krulak later wrote, "Higgins, in his characteristic forthright manner . . . proceeded, at his own expense, to rebuild two . . . Eureka boats." Not only that, but in less than three days, Higgins converted a larger boat into one capable of transporting and unloading an eighteen-ton tank onto a beach. Field tests of both craft proved they would work. The Marine Corps was thrilled. The government gave Higgins a contract to build thousands of his boats. They were used on all the amphibious landings in World War II by both the Army and the Marines from Operation Torch in November 1942 to the invasion of Okinawa in 1945.

Marine General Holland M. Smith stated that the Higgins boat, officially named the LCVP (Landing Craft, Vehicle and Personnel), "contributed more to our common victory than any other single piece of equipment used in the war."

A World War II Higgins boat. (USMC)

IF YOU'D LIKE TO DISCOVER MORE

This was a period where the United States learned about the responsibility of being a world power. Here are a few books that tell more about this important, yet sometimes overlooked, period of American history:

The U.S. Marine Corps At War by Melissa Abramovitz

Eyewitness: World War I by Simon Adams and Andy Crawford

Patton by Martin Blumenson

World War I: A History in Documents by Franz Coetzee

Marine! The Life of Chesty Puller by Burke Davis

Eisenhower by Carlo D'Este

Scholastic Encyclopedia of the United States at War by June English and Thomas D. Jones

Douglas MacArthur: Brilliant General, Controversial Leader by Ann Graham Gaines

A History of Us Book Eight: An Age of Extremes by Joy Hakim

Key Battles of World War I by David Taylor

Dwight D. Eisenhower: Soldier and President by Jeff C. Young

Chapter

4

THE MANTLE OF WORLD POWER

WORLD WAR II

When Nazi Germany attacked Poland on September 1, 1939, the world was plunged into the largest and most terrible war in human history. World War II was fought in every ocean and on every continent except one—only Antarctica was not touched by the conflict—and it disrupted, destroyed, and changed the lives of billions of people.

As in World War I, the United States started out as a neutral nation. That changed on the morning of December 7, 1941, when Japanese airplanes attacked the military bases in and around Pearl Harbor, Hawaii. Though the United States was not as unprepared for war as it was when it entered World War I in 1917, it was still not ready when the Japanese attacked Pearl Harbor. But within a year of that attack, things had dramatically changed. Industry was producing ships, tanks, airplanes, guns, and everything needed to wage war. The services were training millions of men for battle. In August 1942, U.S. Marines launched an offensive against the

Japanese-held island of Guadalcanal in the Pacific Ocean. And, in November 1942, the United States Army landed on the shores of North Africa, the first stage in the ground fight against Germany and Italy.

Although the war did end in a clear-cut military victory for the Allies of the United States, Great Britain, France and the Soviet Union in 1945, true world peace would prove just as elusive as it was when World War I ended. Less than two years after the final shots in World War II were fired, tensions between the Soviet Union and the United States would reach a breaking point, and the world would enter a period of conflict between these two great powers known as the Cold War.

 ## COLD WAR

The Cold War was the name given to the ideological conflict fought on the diplomatic front and through regional wars between the democratic countries led by the United States against the communist nations led by the Soviet Union and Communist China. Historians generally agree that the Cold War started near the end of World War II at the Yalta Conference on February 4–11, 1945, at the resort city of Yalta in the Soviet Union. There the Allies of the United States, Great Britain, and the Soviet Union led by President Franklin Roosevelt, Prime Minister Winston Churchill, and Premier Josef Stalin met to discuss future strategy and the makeup of the post-war world. It was then that regional "spheres of influence" for the Allied nations were unofficially recognized. The suspicions and differences in political philosophies between communist and democractic nations made it inevitable that once the common foes Nazi Germany, Fascist Italy, and Japan were defeated, the two sides would end their alliance. And, in fact, once the war ended in 1945, the old suspicions returned with a vengeance.

The Soviet Union, though a victor, had been savaged by World War II. German armies had invaded the nation, reaching as far as Leningrad (St. Petersburg) in the north, the suburbs of Moscow in the middle, and Stalingrad (Volgograd) in the south. Estimates vary, but at least twenty-seven million civilians died, and more than ten million soldiers were killed. Countless more millions were wounded and left homeless. In contrast, the United States had emerged unscathed and as the most powerful nation in the world—an "arsenal of democracy." In 1945, it was also the only nation with the atomic bomb, a weapon of unprecedented destruction that had annihilated the Japanese cities of Hiroshima and Nagasaki.

Stalin was determined not to allow his country to be so ravaged again. With brutal efficiency, he installed communist governments in the Eastern European nations that the Soviet Army had entered in the advance to Germany. The result was a buffer zone, called an "Iron Curtain" by Prime Minister Winston Churchill, that stretched from the North Sea to the Adriatic Sea. Unwilling to enter into a third World War so quickly after the conclusion of the second, the United States and Great Britain responded through diplomatic efforts and by supplying military and economic aid to such countries as Greece in order to stop a further expansion of communism.

In 1949, the stakes were raised when the Soviet Union successfully exploded its first atomic bomb, producing what amounted to a nuclear standoff. The threat of mutual annihilation in a nuclear war caused the United States and the Soviet Union, and occasionally Communist China, to fight a series of non-nuclear conflicts. The largest of these conflicts occurred in South Korea during the Korean War (1950-1953) which ended in a stalemate and Southeast Asia during the Vietnam War (1965-1972) which ended in a military victory and a diplomatic defeat for the United States.

The economic front, however, was different. It was there that the capitalist systems in the United States and Western Europe would ultimately prove healthier and stronger than the rigid, centralized planning systems administered under communism. The end of communism and the Cold War began on November 9, 1989, with the destruction of the Berlin Wall, a symbol of communist tyranny. This was followed by the collapse of communist governments throughout Eastern Europe. On December 26, 1991, the Union of Soviet Socialist Republics was officially dissolved. On that date, the Cold War finally came to an end. Between 1945 and 1991, for people growing up and living during that period, the threat of the Cold War going "hot" and turning into a global shooting war was an ever-present threat.

 ## KOREAN WAR

The Korean War was one of many conflicts that were the result of irreconcilable political differences between the democracies led by the United States and the communist nations led by the Soviet Union and Communist China. On June 25, 1950, communist North Korea, assisted by supplies and weapons from the Soviet Union, invaded democratic South Korea in a surprise attack.

The Korean War was the first war in history fought by an international organization dedicated to world peace, the United Nations. The United Nations troops, with most of the men and materiél supplied by the United States and under the command of General of the Army Douglas MacArthur, successfully stopped the North Korean army from conquering South Korea. MacArthur then led a campaign that drove the North Koreans back across the 38th parallel, which was the border between North and South Korea. MacArthur then crossed the 38th parallel into North Korea. As his armies neared the Yalu River, which formed the North Korean/Chinese border, in a surprise move Chinese Communist leader Mao Zedong ordered his armies to cross the Yalu River and come to the aid of the North Koreans. President Harry Truman dismissed MacArthur from command on April 11, 1951, because MacArthur publicly advocated an expansion of the war to include the invasion of Communist China, something that President Truman was not prepared to do.

The war settled into a stalemate along the border while the two sides attempted to reach a negotiated settlement. On July 27, 1953, an armistice was signed, effectively ending the war, but to date no peace treaty officially ending the conflict has ever been signed. The Korean War is also known as "The Forgotten War" because it was the first war in U.S. history that did not end in a clear-cut victory for the United States. As a result many Americans attempted to ignore it.

VIETNAM WAR

The Vietnam War was the longest and most traumatic conflict in American history. Although there was never a formal declaration of war, most historians agree that it started on March 8–9, 1965, when President Lyndon Johnson ordered the first combat troops to be deployed at the South Vietnamese port city of Danang. The purpose of America's involvement was to stop the spread of communism in Southeast Asia.

At first, Americans supported the war effort. But as the years of conflict continued with seemingly nothing to show for it, except more and more killed and wounded American troops, people in the United States began turning away from the war. Eventually the unpopularity of the war grew so great that there were massive protests in cities all across the country. Servicemen and women returning from South Vietnam would find themselves attacked by protestors who would curse and throw objects at them. The Paris Peace Accord signed in January 27, 1973, officially ended the war for the United States. Democratic South Vietnam was conquered by communist North Vietnam on April 30, 1975.

In America the physical and emotional scars were profound. America society and some of its most respected institutions had been deeply affected and damaged by the war. Reconciliation with the war officially began on November 10, 1982, with a 56-hour service that marked the dedication of the Vietnam Veterans Memorial in Washington, D.C. The "Wall" lists all of the men and women who died in the conflict—more than 58,000 people.

BENJAMIN O. DAVIS, JR. *Fights to Keep the "Tuskegee Experiment" Alive*

Biography in Brief

BENJAMIN OLIVER DAVIS, JR. (1912-2002) fought in World War II (1939-1945), the Korean War (1950-1953), and the Vietnam War (1965-1973). Davis graduated from West Point in 1936.

In May 1941, he entered Advanced Flying School near Tuskegee Army Air Base. He received his pilot's wings in March 1942. In May 1942, he transferred to the Army Air Corps. In April 1943, he was the commanding officer of the 99th Pursuit Squadron stationed in North Africa and Sicily. In October of that year he assumed command of the 332nd Fighter Group. In May 1944, he was promoted to colonel. Under his command, the 332nd became one of the best fighter groups during the war.

In October 1954, he was promoted to brigadier general, becoming the first African American to become a general in the Air Force. In 1965, he was promoted to lieutenant general and was the chief of staff for the United Nations Command and U.S. Forces in Korea. In 1967, he assumed command of the Thirteenth Air Force stationed at Clark Air Base in the Philippines. On January 22, 1970, Davis retired from the Air Force. On December 9, 1998, Davis was promoted to four-star general.

The following account illustrates how Davis stood up to the racism that threatened his command, and African-American aviators, in World War II.

The tide was turning in the Allies' favor during World War II when, on September 3, 1943, Lieutenant Colonel Benjamin O. Davis, Jr. was relieved of command of the all-black 99th Pursuit Squadron and ordered to return to the United States to assume command of the all-black 332nd Fighter Group. It was a well-earned promotion for a man who had worked hard to prove the 99th could effectively fulfill its missions and fight the enemy in North Africa and the Mediterranean Theater of Operations.

Davis had every right to be proud of the men in his first combat command. In the Pantelleria operation designed to neutralize the enemy-held island in preparation for the invasion of Sicily, the area commander, Colonel J. R. Hawkins, had praised the 99th, writing "heartiest congratulations for the splendid part you played in the Pantelleria show." After Lieutenant Charles "Buster" Hall shot down the first enemy plane, the Allied theater commander himself, General Dwight Eisenhower, along with air force generals James Doolittle and Carl Spaatz, and Air Marshal Arthur Coningham of Britain's Royal Air Force, visited the 99th to personally offer his praise. Eisenhower specifically requested, "I would like to meet the pilot who shot down the [enemy plane]."

The 99th's success, and in fact, the unit's existence, was a testament to the perseverance and ability of Davis and his men. Racism and "Jim Crow" laws that promoted segregation and discrimination were a way of civilian and military life in the United States at the time. Many white leaders had serious doubts about the wartime contribution of blacks. Years earlier, in 1925, the Army War College had issued a report titled "The Use of Negro Manpower in War." It was a multiyear study conducted by the faculty and student body of the Army War College. Ignoring accounts of such units as the 54th Massachusetts Regiment in the Civil War, the 10th Cavalry (the "Buffalo Soldiers") of the Indian Wars, and the 369th Regiment (the "Men of Bronze") in World War I that proved the value of blacks, the study concluded that the intelligence of African-Americans "was lower than that of whites" and that they lacked courage, were superstitious, and were dominated by moral and character weaknesses. This biased report was used to justify the policy of discrimination in the U.S. Army and the Army Air Force.

The outbreak of World War II and the increased manpower needs of all the military services forced the white leadership to change some of the discriminatory regulations. Segregation in the form of separate all-black units with white officers as overall commanders would continue, but, as a result of pressure from civil rights organizations and activists including President Franklin Roosevelt's wife Eleanor, the army agreed to make some changes. One of them came to be known as the "Tuskegee Experiment:" the creation of an all-black air force fighter group that would test to see whether or not blacks could be effective combat pilots. The first unit in this experiment to see action was the 99th Fighter Squadron with Lt. Colonel Benjamin Davis, Jr., as its commanding officer.

Thanks to the praise he and the unit had received during the first three months of combat operations, Davis had every reason to believe that he had proved the success of the "experiment." He was shocked and outraged when he discovered, weeks after his return to the United States, that his superior Colonel William "Spike" Momyer, the commanding officer of the 33rd Fighter Group that included the 99th squadron, had submitted a negative evaluation of the squadron. Momyer, who was an ace with eight confirmed victories, regarded the shooting down of enemy planes as the only true measure of a squadron's achievement and performance. Most of the 99th's missions were hazardous ground support, dive bombing and strafing missions—the type that offered few opportunities to engage enemy planes. Momyer ignored this and wrote, "Based on the performance of the 99th . . . to date, it is my opinion that they are not of the fighting caliber of any squadron in this Group." His report was supported by Momyer's superior, Brigadier General Edwin J. House, who added, "the consensus of opinion seems to be that the negro type has not the proper reflexes to make a first-class pilot." What made matters worse was that Momyer did not follow normal procedure with his evaluation by presenting it first to Davis for his comments. Instead, he bypassed Davis and forwarded it straight to his superior.

These and other similar negative reports made their way up through the air force bureaucracy until they reached the desk of

Lieutenant General Benjamin O. Davis, Jr. (AP/Wide World)

Colonel Davis receives the Distinguished Flying Cross medal from his father, Brigadier General Benjamin O. Davis, Sr. in 1944. The elder Davis was the first African American to reach the rank of general officer. (U.S. Army)

General Henry "Hap" Arnold, commander of the Army Air Force. Arnold contacted his boss, General George C. Marshall, the Army Chief of Staff. Arnold made the recommendation that the 99th be removed from combat, that the 332nd be deployed only for coastal defense, which would mean that it, too, would not see combat, and that the all-black 477th Bomber Group, then in training, be disbanded. Arnold was, in effect, stating that the Tuskegee Experiment was over, and that it was a failure.

Davis's rage was tempered by the seriousness of the situation. The charges were inaccurate, unfair, and racist. Davis was only a lieutenant colonel, yet the stakes were absolute. If he didn't fight back with facts and reasoned rebuttal, everything he and his men had accomplished would be lost. In mid-September 1943, Davis held a press conference at the Pentagon in which he publicly refuted all the negative charges. This seemed to settle the matter in Davis's favor, but then, on October 18, *Time* magazine published an article titled, "Experiment Proved?," that presented a negative picture of the 99th. Because the article contained classified information about the 99th's future role in the war, Davis was convinced that it was a further attempt by individuals in the Army Air Force to discredit blacks and stop the "experiment."

On October 16, 1943, Davis was ordered to meet the War Department Committee on Special Troop Policies, a committee that was responsible for "staff ideas on the employment of Negro troops" during the war. They had already reviewed Colonel Momyer's evaluation and General House's support of it. They wished now to hear Lt. Colonel Davis's side. It would be the committee's recommendation that would help settle the matter once and for all. The future of the program rested on Davis's shoulders. Davis later wrote, "I argued that during the actions against Pantelleria and Sicily, the 99th had performed as well as any new fighter squadron, black or white, could be expected to perform in an unfamiliar environment. I painted a vivid picture of the growth of our combat team from inexperienced fliers to seasoned veterans. . . . I told the committee that if there had been any lack of aggressive spirit in the 99th at first, we had soon made up for it as our pilots gained confidence and began to work successfully as a team. I also pointed out that the squadron had been at a manpower disadvantage; we had only 26 pilots, compared to between 30 and 35 in other squadrons, because expected replacements had not come through until we had been in combat for two months." When he had finished, Davis had addressed every point in Momyer's evaluation and, he hoped, successfully refuted them.

The committee submitted its report, which was classified, and thus kept secret for many years, to General Marshall who would have the final decision in the matter. General Marshall ordered a final operations study be made. When completed it stated in part, "An examination of the record of the 99th Pursuit Squadron reveals no significant general difference between this squadron and the balance of the P-40 squadrons in the Mediterranean Theater Operations."

Davis had taken on the entire bureaucracy and won. As if to underscore the ridiculousness of the charges, Davis observed, "All those who wished to denigrate the quality of the 99th's operations were silenced once and for all by its aerial victories over Anzio . . . in January 1944." An Allied invasion force had landed at the Italian port city of Anzio in an attempt to outflank the German troops in Italy. But the invasion bogged down, and the fighting at Anzio became among the most fierce and difficult in the war. Davis pointed out that among the achievements of the 99th at Anzio, "Eight enemy fighters were downed on 27 January, and four more were destroyed the next day. There would be no more talk of lack of aggressiveness, absence of teamwork, or disintegrating under fire."

> Benjamn Davis, Jr.'s, father, Benjamin Davis, Sr., was America's first African American general. He was promoted to the rank of brigadier general on October 20, 1940.

Six members of the first class of Tuskegee Army Air Force pilot's class in 1942. Davis is the second from left. (U.S. Army)

CHARLES E. "CHUCK" YEAGER *A Flight Officer Group Leader Makes Ace in a Day*

Biography in Brief

CHARLES ELWOOD "CHUCK" YEAGER (1923-present) fought in World War II (1939-1945) and the Vietnam War (1965-1973). He has been called "the fastest man alive" because he was the first man to break the sound barrier in an airplane.

He enlisted in the Army Air Corps in September 1941 and was accepted into the flying sergeant pilot training program in July 1942. In March 1943, Flight Officer Yeager joined the 363rd Fighter Squadron and fought over Europe during World War II.

After World War II, Yeager, now a captain, became a test pilot. On October 14, 1947, he made aviation history when, as the pilot of the X-1, he broke the sound barrier. Yeager later held a series of commands and in 1966, Yeager, now a colonel, returned to combat as the commander of the 405th Fighter Wing during the Vietnam War. In August 1969, he was promoted to brigadier general and on March 1, 1975, he retired from active duty.

The following account is of one dramatic day during World War II when Flight Officer Chuck Yeager shot down five enemy planes, achieving the rare distinction of becoming an "ace in a day."

In 1944, American Army Air Force daylight bombing missions were striking at targets throughout Germany. The German air force—the Luftwaffe—was not as strong as it was when the war started in 1939 because in aerial battle after battle, it became harder and harder for Germany to replace the pilots it lost in combat. Even so, the Luftwaffe was still a dangerous foe. Flying Me-190 and FW-190 fighters, the German pilots were determined to defend their homeland and stop the American bombers from destroying their country.

Flight Officer Chuck Yeager was a 21-year-old member of the Eighth Air Force's 357th Fighter Group. Based in England, the group flew the hottest American fighter plane in the war, the P-51 Mustang. Flight officers were rare in the Army Air Force; they were the most junior of officers, ranking below a second lieutenant. Although Yeager was the most junior officer in the group because of his rank, he was one of the most senior pilots when it came to experience. Not only had he flown many combat missions, he had also been shot down over enemy-occupied France, evaded capture and returned to England. It came as a surprise to Yeager when he was told that on October 12, 1944, he would be a group leader on a mission escorting bombers. Yeager was unconcerned about the fact that he'd be leading into battle men who were lieutenants and captains. As he later said regarding such assignments, "Basically, in World War II, rank didn't mean anything. It was your ability as a leader." Instead, he said the prayer all pilots used when put in tight situations, "Lord, just don't let me screw up."

Aerial combat in World War II was a lot different than it is now. Today, using radar to guide them, pilots can fight each other and not be in visual contact. During World War II, not only did opposing pilots get into visual contact, they sometimes literally came in physical contact as well in chaotic, aerial "dogfights." Imagine a swarm of angry bees, only these "bees" are fighter planes locked in a swirling melee that would begin tens of thousands of feet above the surface of the earth and go all the way down to the "deck" as the ground was called. That's a

Captain Charles Elwood "Chuck" Yeager. (USAF)

World War II dogfight.

For mutual protection, American pilots fought in escalating groups of two. The basic unit was the two-plane "element" composed of a pilot who did the hunting and shooting of the enemy and his wing man who kept pace, flying beside "riding

Chuck Yeager standing beside the X-1 Glamorous Glennis *in which he broke the sound barrier.* (USAF)

shotgun"—keeping a lookout for any enemy planes that might try to attack. The next grouping is the four-plane "flight" composed of two elements. The next largest is the squadron composed of four flights. Then there is the "group" which contains three squadrons. Once the chaos of a dogfight started, it was impossible for groups and squadrons to remain together. That was why the element was so important. As Yeager explained, "When you got into combat, you broke up into an element, a leader and his wing man. You never went below that . . . because without a wing man you don't crawl up behind some enemy and start shooting, because some guy will come in behind you and hammer you. So the wing man always stays in contact with you . . . and watches his tail and your tail."

A typical mission day started early. Pilots were awake by 5:30 A.M. Shaving was done with cold water because usually hot water wasn't available. Despite this discomfort, men made sure they shaved as close as possible. Because they'd be flying in oxygen-thin atmosphere, pilots had to wear oxygen masks. Since they'd be wearing the tight-fitting masks for almost six hours, any leftover stubble would cause severe chafing. After getting cleaned and dressed, the men would exit their barracks and assemble in the group briefing hut where the group leader would stand on stage and present the information about the day's mission. On October 12, Flight Officer Chuck Yeager was the man on stage briefing the 48 men he would lead into combat. Yeager also had a special guest that morning. As he later said, "Now, when I was briefing the group, I was up on the stage and we had the maps [showing the flight route, rendezvous point with the bombers, and the target], and I went through the engine start times and the takeoff times and things like this."

As Yeager was going through his briefing, Lieutenant General James H. "Jimmy" Doolittle, commanding officer of the Eighth Air Force, was in the audience. At one point during the briefing Yeager later recalled that General Doolittle turned to the group commander, a colonel, and asked, "'What's that kid up there got on his collar?' The colonel said, 'A flight officer bar.' I don't think General Doolittle had ever seen one for he said, 'That's lower than a second lieutenant, isn't it?' The colonel said, 'Yes, it is.' Doolittle said, 'What's he doing leading a

Chuck Yeager in one of the planes that he flew during his days as a test pilot. (USAF)

group?' The colonel said, 'Well, he's about as good as we've got.'"

Their mission that day called for Yeager's P-51 group, composed of the 362nd, 363rd, and 364th squadrons, to protect a group of B-24 Liberator bombers that were going to attack the German port city of Bremen. After the fighters rendezvoused with the bombers over the Netherlands, Yeager positioned the 362nd and 364th squadrons for close-in protection of the bombers. Then he proceeded to fly his squadron, the 363rd, well in advance of the bombers in order to intercept any approaching enemy planes. Yeager had one big advantage in doing this: his extraordinarily keen eyesight that he and the other pilots called "combat vision." Of it Yeager said, "You focus out to infinity and back, searching a section of sky each time." On this day what he saw were 22 German Me-109 fighters waiting to pounce on the approaching bombers. Because he was able to see the enemy before they could see him, Yeager was able to maneuver his squadron into an attacking position above the Me-109s and with the sun at the P-51s back. This made it almost impossible for the enemy pilots to see the P-51s until the attack had started. As soon as he got his squadron into position, he attacked.

Of that combat, Yeager recalled, "I came in behind their tail-end Charlie and was about to begin hammering him,

SILVER STAR: A medal awarded in the name of the President of the United States for gallantry in action against the enemy.

when he suddenly broke left and ran into his wingman. They both bailed out. It was almost comic, scoring two quick victories without firing a shot. . . . By now, all the airplanes in that sky . . . were spinning and diving in a wild, wide-open dogfight. I blew up a 109 from six hundred yards—my third victory—when I turned around and saw another angling in behind me. Man, I pulled back on my throttle so . . . hard I nearly stalled, rolled up and over, came in behind and under him, kicking right rudder and simultaneously firing. I was directly underneath the guy, less than fifty feet, and I opened up that 109 as if it were a can of Spam. That made four. A moment later I [shot down another] in a steep dive; I pulled up at about 1,000 feet; he went straight into the ground."

With the fifth plane shot down, Yeager had the distinction of accomplishing one of the rarest achievements in air war, becoming an "ace in a day." When they returned to base that day, the rest of the pilots threw a party in celebration, and later, he would be officially recognized for his achievement with the award of a Silver Star medal.

Glamorous Glen III, *the third P-51 Mustang that Yeager named after his future wife, Glennis. Note the twelve Nazi flags just below the canopy, signifying that Yeager had shot down twelve enemy fighters.* (USAF)

GEORGE S. PATTON *In the Shadow of an Illustrious Father*

When Captain George Patton arrived in South Korea and reported to 40th Division headquarters in February 1953, he told assistant division commander Brigadier General Gordon V. Rogers, who had known Patton's family for years, "General Rogers, I'm not asking for any favors, and please understand that I'll do exactly as I'm told. . . . On the other hand, I came to Korea to fight and I hope you will give me that chance."

Patton's request was soon granted, and he found himself in command of a tank company positioned along the Demilitarized Zone (DMZ) between North and South Korea. This was the period of peace negotiations between representatives of the American-led United Nations and the North Koreans, but that didn't mean that combat had completely ended. Periodically skirmishes would occur, the result of scouting raids on both sides. Otherwise the war had settled into static warfare where no offensive was planned. Static warfare is among the most grueling types of warfare that soldiers face. Troops are required to remain in defensive fortifications and stay alert for any enemy incursion. Movement is limited to reconnaissance patrols. The biggest challenge for a commander is not so much how to repulse an enemy attack as it is how to keep his men from getting bored and depressed.

Patton soon discovered, upon taking command of his company, that the morale of his troops had hit rock bottom. Also, Patton saw that his men were suspicious of him. They knew that he was the son of the famous General Patton of World War II, and that like his father, he was a graduate of West Point. Captain Patton saw in their eyes that many believed he was there only long enough to get the frontline experience needed for promotion, perhaps even a medal, before leaving for a warm, safe, and secure staff job far away from the wet, cold, and miserable DMZ. Patton knew he had his work cut out for him if he was going to get that attitude changed.

He later wrote, "Remembering the motto that God gave a person two ears and one mouth and to use them in that proportion, I went about the business of talking to people

Biography in Brief
GEORGE PATTON (1923-2004), the son of General George S. Patton, Jr., fought in the Korean War (1950-1953) and the Vietnam War (1965-1973) where he served three tours of duty. Shortly after graduation from West Point in 1946, Lieutenant Patton was sent to Germany where he assisted in the Berlin Airlift crisis (1948).

Promoted to captain, Patton was posted to South Korea in 1953 where he commanded a tank company along the Demilitarized Zone. In 1962 Patton, now a major, was ordered to South Vietnam at a time when the United States was only providing military advisors through the Military Assistance Advisory Group (MAAG). Promoted to lieutenant colonel, he returned to the United States in 1963 where he commanded a tank battalion. Patton returned to South Vietnam in 1967, and in 1968, he was promoted to colonel. In 1970, he was promoted to brigadier general, and in 1972, to major general. Patton retired from active duty in 1980. He died on June 27, 2004.

The following account is of his first combat command in Korea. Captain George Patton arrived in South Korea in early 1953, when the war was in its final stages. Although combat was limited, he faced many challenges. The biggest one was how he, the son and namesake of the famous World War II general, could earn the respect of the men under his command and make a name for himself.

Major General George S. Patton (AP/Wide World)

concerning what was both right and wrong [in the unit]."

Patton knew that little things taken for granted in the United States, including mail from home, a hot meal, clean clothes, dry socks, and hot showers, become very important to soldiers stationed in faraway and foreign lands. As he visited his men, he asked them many questions about mail delivery, the food, and other subjects including furloughs and enemy contact. The answers he received gave him much to think about. After four days of studying the situation, Patton listed his problems. The men were bored and tired; there was no mess tent where men behind the lines could eat; soldiers on the front line did not receive hot meals, and mail service was poor. He also saw that his subordinate officers were content to stay inside their sheltered command posts while the men under their command remained at their front-line stations, which were cold and uncomfortable because they were open to the weather.

Captain Patton decided that the most important immediate need—and the one where he could demonstrate the quickest that he truly cared about the welfare of the men under his command—was by personally serving hot food to his men on the front line. Patton called in his executive officer, his second in command, and told him that he wanted the troops on the front line fed a hot meal. The "exec" protested, "Sir, I think that's impossible; there's too much exposure." What the exec meant was that, even though there was a truce, the North Koreans didn't always obey it. He was afraid that the North Koreans would try to shoot anyone, especially an officer, moving along the front line. Patton thanked his exec for his concern and then commanded, "Not only are we going to do it, but I will be there personally. We'll start in the morning with the lunch meal and we'll finish when we finish."

At 9:30 the following morning, Patton, riding in a jeep, led a mess truck to his tank crews stationed along the DMZ. The men were stunned. Such a thing had never before happened to them. At 4:00 P.M., Patton was dishing out a meal to the last tank crew. He told them, "I'm sorry this is so late, it's not very hot, but it is from the heart." One of the men replied, "Captain, this is the first hot meal I have had in three weeks. I understand it is not very good, and I understand it is cold, but I appreciate

Troopers in Korea warming up over a stove created from a tin container. Korean winters were bitterly cold and frostbite and trench foot were common dangers for men who had to spend long hours in foxholes or front line trenches. (U.S. Army)

FURLOUGH: In the military, an authorized vacation.

115

Simple things, such as drying laundry in the winter, become challenges when in the field, as this soldier discovers. (U.S. Army)

what you are doing."

Patton later led the company in some limited battles against the North Koreans before returning back to the United States in March 1954. By the time his tour ended, he had earned the respect of his men. He did, however, fulfill one suspicion his men had of him: he did get a medal, the Silver Star for his service in South Korea. Because Patton had taken the time to care for his men, it was a medal he had rightly earned. Major Allen Weinfield, who was responsible for writing the ratings for subordinate officers in the division, wrote, "[Patton] has great ability and succeeds in instilling confidence, pride, and skill into the officers and men under his command."

Although he would forever be identified with his illustrious father, by the time he retired in 1980 with the rank of major general, George Patton would realize his goal of carving out a successful military career based on his own merits.

Although being the son of a famous general occasionally was a burden, there were times when it gave Patton unique experiences and perspectives. In a speech, Patton once recounted, "I was bounced on General Pershing's knee. I groomed Eisenhower's horses. I saw Douglas MacArthur come into my house as a small boy. I walked General Marshall's hunting dog."

COLIN LUTHER POWELL *An ARVN Advisor in the A Shau Valley*

In 1963, the conflict in Vietnam had yet to become the divisive war that almost tore apart the United States. Before 1965, and the deployment of combat forces in South Vietnam (officially the Republic of Vietnam), America's military presence was composed of approximately 16,000 military advisors. Their role was to train the Army of the Republic of Vietnam (ARVN) to defend the country from the communist guerilla insurgents known as the Viet Cong and from attack by the People's Army of Vietnam (PAVN) from communist North Vietnam. Captain Colin Powell was ordered to serve as the advisor to the 2nd Battalion, 3rd Infantry Regiment of the 1st Division located in the A Shau Valley near the border with Laos. Powell was paired with the commanding officer of the 2nd Battalion, Captain Vo Cong Hieu. The Viet Cong used the A Shau Valley as a travel route to their objective: The coast towns where they planned to inspire a revolt against the South Vietnamese government. The mission of the 2nd Battalion was to intercept and capture and kill any Viet Cong they found in the valley. Powell later wrote, "I tried to blend in with the ARVN. I wore the same uniform and carried the same pack. I pinned my captain's bars onto the front of my blouse, concealed by my gear. And, for once, my color provided an advantage. I was color-coordinated with the Vietnamese and by slouching became virtually indistinguishable from Hieu's men."

Powell accompanied the troops on their patrols through the thick jungle. The tropical heat was intense. He and the men had to constantly drink water and repeatedly take salt tablets to replace the salt in their bodies that was lost through their sweat. It was hard work moving through the jungle. The terrain was rocky and slippery; it was a constant struggle to pass through the dense vegetation. Clouds of biting insects followed them everywhere. The thing that Powell considered the worst was the leeches. Regardless of what the men did, somehow the leeches would manage to work their way through the gear and clothing and latch onto the skin. "We stopped as often as ten times a day to get rid of them," he later wrote. The two most common and

Biography in Brief
COLIN LUTHER POWELL (1937-present) fought in the Vietnam War (1965-1973) and oversaw Operation Just Cause (1989) and Operations Desert Shield/Desert Storm (1990-1991). A graduate of the City College of New York Reserve Officer Training Course, he entered the army in 1958. Because of his high marks, he received a regular army commission instead of a reserve commission.

Powell served two tours in Vietnam. His first, as an advisor, began on Christmas Day 1962. In 1968, he served on staff postings in the Americal Division.

In 1979, he was promoted to brigadier general. In 1983, he was promoted to major general and became the senior military advisor to Secretary of Defense Caspar Weinberger. In 1986, he was promoted to lieutenant general. Later that year, he became Deputy National Security Advisor, and in 1987, the National Security Advisor.

In 1989, he was promoted to general. Later, becoming the twelfth Chairman of the Joint Chiefs of Staff—the youngest officer, the first African American, and the first ROTC graduate to hold the position. After serving two terms as chairman, Powell retired from the army. From 2001 to 2005, Powell served as Secretary of State, the first African American to hold that office.

This account is from 1963 when Powell, a captain, was a military advisor to a South Vietnamese army unit.

Powell shared two things with his predecessor George Marshall. Neither of them attended West Point, and both of them became Secretary of State.

Colin Powell, official Secretary of State photograph. (State Department)

efficient methods of getting rid of leeches was to use insect repellent or to burn them off, usually with the lit end of a cigarette.

The Viet Cong constantly ambushed the ARVN patrols. As required, Powell was usually well back in the column of men. Typically, he would hear a quick burst of gunfire from a Viet Cong AK-47 assault rifle, a few return shots from the ARVN, and then silence. Many times when he reached the site of the ambush he would find the point man of the patrol either killed or wounded. Rarely would they find the body of a Viet Cong. In an effort to reduce casualties among the lead patrol, Powell offered Captain Hieu a solution, body armor. The United States had sent in supplies of "armored" vests composed of overlapping and crisscrossed layers of densely woven nylon that were designed to stop the penetration of most small arms ammunition including the bullets fired by an AK-47. At first, Captain Hieu resisted. He pointed out that the vests were cumbersome, heavy, and hot. Also, they were designed for American bodies, and thus were awkward on the much smaller Vietnamese soldier. For almost two months, Captain Hieu refused to consider issuing the vests. Finally, after yet another one of his men lay wounded on the jungle floor after a Viet Cong ambush, he agreed.

Powell requisitioned the vests, and they were put on the squad assigned to lead the next patrol. Less than an hour into the patrol, Powell heard the abrupt firing of an AK-47, a pause, a sharp burst of return fire followed by silence. Typically Powell would then hear screams or moans, and when he arrived on the scene he would find himself facing a wounded ARVN point man. This time though, he was surprised to hear laughter. A couple of ARVN soldiers returned from the point and gestured for him to come forward quickly. When he reached the head of the column, he found the point man laughing nervously. As Powell later wrote, "He was wearing an armored vest with a dent punched in the back, a flattened bullet still embedded in the thick nylon layering."

In broken English the man explained that he was blazing a trail through the jungle when the ambush occurred. He had turned to signal to the lead squad the location of the ambush when he was struck in the back by a Viet Cong bullet. Powell pried the bullet out of the vest. The flattened round was passed to the soldiers who stared at it and the vest in awe. The troops' respect for Powell increased dramatically; he had proved himself an important leader. Of course, such leadership also carried increased responsibility, and as he later noted, "The only problem now was that during the next supply delivery, I could not get enough vests for all the men who wanted them."

Powell spent six months in the "boonies" as the jungles and rural areas of South Vietnam were called. Powell was wounded, stepping on a Viet Cong punji stake. After recovering from his wound he served as an assistant advisor on the operations staff of the 1st Division. He completed his first tour and left South Vietnam in late 1963 at a time when the U.S. government was confident that its mission to prevent a communist takeover was

A soldier taking a bath in South Vietnam with the help of some friends. (U.S. Army)

U.S. Army advisors sharing a meal with their South Vietnamese army soldiers. (U.S. Army)

General Colin Powell, U.S. Army (Department of Defense)

succeeding, but Powell had his doubts. Despite this, he still believed in the importance of being in South Vietnam. He also believed that the mission was much larger than the leaders in Washington, D.C., thought. During the time when he was on staff in the South Vietnamese city of Hue, he later recalled that, "An analyst had asked me, as a guy who had been in the field, what the job was going to take. 'It'll take,' I said, 'half a million men to succeed.'"

WILMA VAUGHT *A Victory over Fear*

There were "two wars" being fought in Vietnam-the "shooting war" against the communist Viet Cong and the North Vietnamese Army, and the "paper war" against the bureaucrats in Washington, D.C., led by Secretary of Defense Robert McNamara who demanded an accounting for every bullet, barrel, and body. In 1968, Major Wilma Vaught received orders posting her to a staff position at MACV headquarters. Unlike her first tour in 1966, on Guam, an island thousands of miles away from the fighting, this time she would be stationed in a war zone. Although women were legally barred from serving in combat commands in the Vietnam War, that did not mean they wouldn't be exposed to danger. As she later recalled, the feeling she had when she received her orders was that, "I wouldn't be coming back alive . . . that this was going to be it for me."

Viet Cong terrorist incidents occurred throughout South Vietnam. These terrorist incidents were demoralizing as they could, and did, happen anytime and anywhere. Major Vaught arrived in Saigon in October 1968. The communist Tet offensive was over, but its memory was very fresh. The U.S. Embassy in Saigon had been attacked during the offensive, and the compound walls still bore the scars of that assault, a mute reminder that no place in South Vietnam was truly safe. She observed that, "There were sandbags everywhere." Her personal quarters were located in downtown Saigon, just three blocks behind the Presidential Palace, but she soon discovered that some people refused to live off base because of the potential for danger.

When she reported for duty at MACV headquarters and was briefed by the officer she was about to replace, she discovered that her duty, the preparation of quarterly cost saving reports that would get forwarded to the Secretary of Defense, would be very small and take little time. Her task was simply to gather and organize information from other departments and essentially list what was used, how it was used, and the effectiveness of its use. As she later recalled, "And that's all I was supposed to do. I then asked the person I was replacing, 'After you finish the report, what do you do for the next three months?' And he said,

Biography in Brief
WILMA L. VAUGHT (1930-present) served two tours in the Vietnam War (1965-1973). She was commissioned a second lieutenant in January 1957. In 1966, Captain Vaught served her first tour in the Vietnam War. She became the first woman to deploy with a Strategic Air Command operational unit when she was the executive officer and chief of the Management Analysis Division, 4133rd Provisional Bombardment Wing stationed in Guam.

Her second tour of duty in the Vietnam War began in October 1968. Now a major, she was stationed in Saigon where she was a member of the Office of the Deputy Chief of Staff, Comptroller, Military Assistance Command, Vietnam (MACV).

On September 8, 1980, Vaught was promoted to brigadier general, the first woman in the career field of comptroller to achieve star rank. In 1982 she was the senior woman military representative to the Defense Advisory Committee on Women in the Services, and in 1983, she also served as Chairperson of the NATO Women in the Allied Forces Committee, holding both positions until her retirement in August 1985.

The following account occurred during her second tour in the Vietnam War. She was assigned a staff position and stationed in the South Vietnamese capital of Saigon, There she experienced an emotion frontline soldiers know well: fear.

Major Wilma Vaught at her desk at Military Assistance Command Vietnam Headquarters (MACV HQ), Saigon, Vietnam, 1969. (WIMSA)

'You just wait for the next three months to go by.' I wasn't going to just sit there for the tour and do something four times and that's it. I started looking for things to do." She successfully added more duties and responsibilities, spearheading investigations into the use of the defoliant Agent Orange and suspected black market activities in petroleum facilities.

Occasionally, she would be reminded of the random and impersonal nature of the war when, in one instance, ". . . a rocket attack occurred a couple blocks away from where I was." Even though she had a premonition of death before arriving in South Vietnam, she succeeded in keeping busy so that the possibility of her own mortality did not become an issue for her. One day that changed. She was talking to a lieutenant colonel with whom she had been working. The lieutenant colonel was a man with more than 20 years of service, and his tour in South Vietnam was almost over. The slang expression was that he was "short" or "a short timer." Since he had less than a week before he would be leaving for the United States, she asked him how he was feeling.

Brigadier General Wilma Vaught, USAF. (WIMSA)

She recalled, "He said, 'Well, I hate to admit this, but I am so afraid that I won't live to get to go home that I have cleaned out everything in my BOQ [Bachelor Officer's Quarters], and I am sleeping in one of these cots here in the [MACV] building so that all I have to do on the day I leave is walk across the street to the airport and get on that plane and leave.'" Later that week, on the day of his departure, the lieutenant colonel took his bag, marched across the tarmac to the awaiting airplane, and flew home.

Meanwhile the lieutenant colonel's confession had caused Major Vaught to do some thinking. As she later said, "My reaction was that I wasn't going to live with fear." When she became "short," she said, "I hadn't been afraid, and I decided I wasn't going to live with fear. So I scheduled a trip to the Army base at Long Binh where I had worked as a liaison with some people there to say farewell. The distance was about 25 miles. It was just one car with me and a driver. We didn't carry any weapons. I wasn't going to be driving through an area that was necessarily felt to be a hazard, but a Viet Cong attack could come anywhere and at anytime. There were people [at MACV] who wouldn't drive [on the road to Long Binh] for anything."

Once everything was arranged, she and her driver took off. During the trip, Vaught made an additional stop along the way. "One of the highlights of the trip," she said, "was a cemetery that was sort of the Vietnam equivalent to the Arlington cemetery. We drove to it and I visited it. I'm probably one of the few Americans at that point in time who had ever seen that."

The trip was completed without incident. But Major Vaught had not concluded her confrontation with fear. The Cholon district of Saigon was reputed to be a center of Viet Cong activity. It also had a restaurant, the House of Seven Beefs. "Now, I didn't know what the seven beefs were, whether they were cow, or dog, or cat, or whatever," she recalled. "But I said that's where I want my farewell party to be. And that was where my farewell party was."

When the day came in 1969 for her to pack her bag and return to "the world," as the United States was called, she left her BOQ near the Presidential Palace, got on the plane, and departed, all without fear.

Major Wilma Vaught at the entrance to her office at MACV HQ, Saigon, Vietnam, 1969. (WIMSA)

CAROL MUTTER *A Lesson in Leadershi;p*

Biography in Brief

CAROL MUTTER (1945-present) was the first woman in the Marine Corps to reach the rank of major general and lieutenant general. In 1967, she was commissioned a second lieutenant.

From 1969-1972, she was a platoon commander and instructor for women noncommissioned officers, women officer candidates, and women basic lieutenants. From 1973-1984 when she rose from captain to lieutenant colonel, she served in a variety of commands, including the 1st Marine Aircraft Wing in Okinawa, Japan. In 1988, Colonel Mutter joined the U.S. Space Command and was responsible for the operation of the Space Command Commander in Chief's Command Center.

In 1991, Mutter became a brigadier general. In 1992, she became the commanding general of the 3rd Force Service Support Group, Okinawa, and the first woman to command a major deployable unit in the field.

In June 1994, she was promoted to major general, and on September 1, 1996, lieutenant general. She retired on January 1, 1999.

The following account is from the period 1969-1972, when she was a platoon commander at Quantico and training women officer candidates to be Marines.

When Carol Mutter was commissioned a first lieutenant in the Marine Corps in 1967, the role of women in the military was different. It was a time when choosing the military was not high on the list of career options for women. Jobs within the services were few because of the restrictive laws and policies in place at the time. "The laws really reflected the spirit of the time," she recalled. "You could not have children and stay in the military. There were no women in combat or combat support units, including Marine aviation. So jobs were limited." Also, because they were not assigned to units that would be sent to combat—known as deployable units—women did not receive the full measure of field training that women receive now. In the Marine Corps the highest rank for women was colonel, and only one woman was allowed to hold that rank.

In fact the law denied general officer status to women in all branches of the military. Nonetheless, Mutter decided to join, picking the Marines because, she said, she wanted to be among "the best."

Mutter was a 24-year-old first lieutenant stationed at the Marine base at Quantico, Virginia, in 1969. Located approximately 35 miles south of Washington, D.C., along the Potomac River, the Quantico Marine Base surrounds the town of Quantico on three sides, the fourth side being the Potomac River. Civilian protests against the Vietnam War in Southeast Asia were few at the time. Later they would increase, and anti-military sentiment would become so pronounced that Mutter later said that she didn't wear her uniform when she was off base, particularly when she had to travel (in order to avoid confrontations at airports).

Training of all women commissioned officers is done at Quantico. Today, the training is integrated, although the living quarters are still separate. In the early 1970s, however, training was done separately. At that time, women underwent training in facilities along the banks of the Potomac River, three miles from where the men were trained.

In late 1968, she was notified that starting in January 1969 she would receive a two-year assignment as a platoon leader responsible for training female Marine Corps officer candidates and basic lieutenants. During this assignment, she was also an instructor and platoon commander for leadership classes for both officers and noncommissioned officers or NCOs.

She recalled, "I was a little bit apprehensive. As far as I knew it was a very tough job and would be very difficult and demanding. I wasn't sure if I was really well prepared, but I also knew it was a great opportunity." At that time there were approximately 3,000 female enlisted members, and only about 300 women officers in the Corps. With such small numbers, pressure to perform was intense. Earlier, during her training at Officer Candidate School, she recalled her instructors saying, "We were going to be living in a goldfish bowl. . . . So what they impressed on us was the professionalism that was necessary." Performing well with this constant additional pressure would certainly help when it came time for promotion.

Mutter faced two distinct challenges related to the training. "Officer candidates and basic lieutenants were, of course, trained differently," she said. "Training officer candidates is essentially a screening process, whereas officers (basic lieutenants) are already members of the Marine Corps . . . so the focus during officer training is on making them better leaders."

Mutter had learned early the value of relying on her noncommissioned officers (NCOs). Occasionally a sergeant will be promoted to a commissioned officer status, but that is rare. Generally, second lieutenants, male and female, are almost always unfamiliar with their assignments; the smart ones learn very quickly to ask their NCOs questions. "In fact, the sergeants respected you more when you asked questions," Mutter said. "If you, as an officer, acted as if you knew everything because you were an officer, or appeared unwilling to ask questions, your NCOs lost respect for you." Female noncommissioned officers faced some challenges that Mutter was very sensitive to. Female NCOs were a small minority within a minority. "The corporal and the sergeant are the first level of supervision in the Marine Corps and the leaders who really make things happen," she said. The backbone of the Corps, "they are out there on the 'tip of the spear,' as we call it. The sergeants are the ones with experi-

1st Lieutenant Carol Mutter, left, in the Data Processing Office at Camp Pendleton, California, August 1970. (Carol Mutter)

Mutter prepares for a familiarization ride in an F/A-18 in Japan, 1996. (Carol Mutter)

ence and who get the work done. Officers rely on the NCOs to conduct the training of recruits and Marines. . . . Some had the unfortunate experience of being with male Marines who just didn't want to have a woman in a position of authority over them. I said, 'Do your homework, do your job, act like you belong here, and it will work out.'"

It was advice that Mutter followed herself as she took on the responsibility of platoon commander for her first class of officer candidates. The class was a typical mix of ethnic and social-economic groups in their early to mid-twenties. "There were also in the group," she said, "some former enlisted women from the Marines, and of course they stood out immediately because they already knew how to be a Marine and they had already told themselves that they were going to be top performers."

As the program progressed, Mutter and her staff of instructors would keep individual daily records of each officer candidate, noting on paper any problems or potential problems called "chits." There was no trigger level of chit accumulation that caused the officer candidate to be called in for a private meeting. "Every case is different," Mutter said. "There's no set formula because leadership by definition is very individual. It depends on each individual's case and circumstance. There is a myriad of factors that go into the process."

As a platoon commander, Mutter was with the women officers 16 hours a day, constantly observing. "You could see right from the start some couldn't handle the physical fitness training, some had difficulty with their weight. There were academic and other problems. Through observation and counseling sessions, it very soon became obvious which candidates were going to be able to overcome their personal hurdles and which weren't."

When, after all attempts to assist failed, and the time came to tell the officer candidate she would be dropped from the Marines, Mutter said, "My feelings were one of almost dread. I don't know of a better word for it. It's a confrontational situation. You know it's not going to be pretty; it's not going to be fun. . . . You have to convince somebody of something that they don't want to be convinced of."

One of the most agonizing cases was with a failing officer candidate whose family had a history in the military. "Her dad was a Marine," Mutter said. "Ever since she was five years old she wanted to be a Marine. This was always something that she had worked for and facing the fact that she wasn't going to be a Marine was a very difficult thing."

Though Mutter had compassion for this officer candidate and others who had tried their best but couldn't achieve their goal, she realized that the decision she was making was best for both the individual and for the Corps. "Being a good leader is taking care of the men and women that you lead," she said. "But that doesn't mean allowing them to slack off and ignore requirements. It means insuring that they perform to the standards required by the institution, because if they're not, that will eventually catch up with them."

The value of her developing tenacity and leadership ability to deal with tough decisions was revealed to her years later. "I saw a Marine who had been in for many years," she remembered. "Folks had tended to help him along because he was a good guy and could do good work. But he had some issues in meeting Marine Corps standards. Earlier in that Marine's career his leaders should have confronted his shortcomings and worked with him to overcome them; instead those training officers thought they were 'taking care of him' by overlooking his failings." The result, Mutter recalled was that the Marine "was dragging the unit down. It affected the morale of the unit, the ability of the unit to do its job."

He wore the uniform, but as she observed about those she trained, "Not everybody can be or should stay a Marine."

Lieutenant General Carol Mutter, USMC (Marine Corps)

FRED FRANKS *The "Hot Blue Flame" of Trust*

Biography in Brief

FREDERICK MELVIN FRANKS, JR. (1936-present) fought in the Vietnam War (1965-1973) and Operations Desert Shield/Desert Storm (1990-1991). He graduated from West Point in 1959.

In August 1969, Franks, now a major, served with the 11th Armored Cavalry Regiment ("Blackhorse") in South Vietnam. Severely wounded in action on May 5, 1970, Franks was evacuated to the United States and hospitalized at the Valley Forge General Hospital near Phoenixville, Pennsylvania.

Because his wounded left leg was not healing properly, it was amputated below the knee in January 1971. In 1982, Franks, now a colonel, once again returned to the 11th Armored Cavalry Regiment, this time as its commanding officer. In 1984 he was promoted to brig. general. In 1989 he was promoted to lieutenant general and commanding officer of VII Corps, which he commanded during Operations Desert Shield/Desert Storm. On August 7, 1991, he was promoted to the rank of full general and appointed commander of TRADOC. Franks retired from the Army in 1994.

The following account is of an event in the Vietnam War when Franks' career almost came to an end in a region of Cambodia known as the Fishhook in what the military calls "a meeting engagement" with a unit of the North Vietnamese Army.

The North Vietnamese Army had established a major sanctuary in the Cambodian provincial capital of Snoul, near the border of South Vietnam. For many years, Military Assistance Command, Vietnam (MACV), operated under a presidential order not to attack these and other sanctuaries in Cambodia. During those years U.S. troops attacking Viet Cong and North Vietnamese Army (NVA) troops near the border could not follow up and destroy the retreating enemy once it crossed the boundary into Cambodia. The result, of course, was that once the communists reached the sanctuary, their wounded could recover, they could rest, receive reinforcements and supplies, and train without fear of attack. In 1969, that ban was lifted and the sanctuaries were now fair game.

On April 30, 1970, Major Fred Franks, an operations officer in the Blackhorse cavalry, learned he would be among those leading an attack that would be one of the first blows struck against the enemy. Their objective was an important North Vietnamese Army supply base and sanctuary near the provincial capital of Snoul. On the morning of May 1, the Blackhorse launched the attack and crossed the border into Cambodia. The advance was rapid, and for the next few days, the NVA retreated fighting small battles. But on May 4, when they realized that the Americans were not stopping, and were near the outskirts of their sanctuary at Snoul, they prepared to fight.

That night Second Squadron Commander Lt. Colonel Grail Brookshire and Major Franks were given their objectives by their commanding officer, Colonel Donn Starry. They would be attacking an airfield east of the town. Seizing it would greatly assist resupply of the Blackhorse because the airfield was large enough to accept the C-130 Hercules transport planes. They planned to attack from the south, charging through a rubber plantation that stood between them and their objective.

The next morning, the attack stunned the surprised NVA defenders and, despite the fact that the advancing Americans were in an exposed position as they crossed the airfield, they encountered only sporadic fire. Franks knew that would quickly change. To keep the enemy off balance they needed intelligence about the location and size of the enemy defenses around and near the airfield, and they needed it fast. A bunker near an anti-aircraft gun had revealed some NVA troops still alive. Franks ran over to the bunker to see if he could get the information they needed from one of the trapped communist soldiers. Rocky, the squadron's Vietnamese interpreter, was trying to convince two men still in the bunker to come out and talk. Franks grabbed a log on top of the bunker, determined to open it up and get the NVA soldiers out. Suddenly one of the NVA soldiers inside threw out a grenade. Franks didn't see the grenade, but Colonel Starry, who was at the bunker as well, did and leaped forward in an attempt to knock Franks out of the way.

The grenade exploded. Fragments from the grenade peppered Starry's face, chest, and abdomen. Fortunately, Starry was not seriously wounded. The same could not be said for Franks. Despite Starry's attempt, Major Franks had suffered the brunt of the blast. He had wounds all over his body. His left foot and lower leg were a mass of blood and pulp. Immediately a call went out on the radio for a "dustoff"—an evacuation of wounded by helicopter. At the same time, the men of Second Squadron, who hadn't been wounded, angrily finished off the defiant NVA soldiers in the bunker.

Within minutes, a helicopter had arrived for the dustoff. Nearby NVA antiaircraft guns fired at the helicopter as the wounded were loaded and flown to safety. In less than 15 minutes, both Colonel Starry and Major Franks were gone. At the Army base in Long Binh, Franks asked a doctor if he was going to lose his foot.

"Nah," the doctor replied. "Six months and you'll be up and around doing duty."

From Long Binh, Major Franks was flown to Camp Zama Hospital in Japan. There he asked Dr. Jeff Malke the same question.

"You don't want to hear this," Dr. Malke answered, "but six months from now, you're going to decide you'd be better off without that foot. But you're probably going to have to go through a battle to decide that yourself. . . . Major, that is just

Lieutenant General Fred Franks in the Middle East during Operation Desert Storm in 1991. (John D. Gresham)

The "Huey"—officially the UH-1 Iroquois—was the workhorse of the Vietnam War. It was used for everything from troop and supply transport and medical evacuation of wounded troops to aerial gunship support in combat operations. It was used for so many things during the conflict that it became a symbol of the Vietnam War. (U.S. Army)

not a good-looking leg and foot."

Franks underwent a series of surgeries to repair his limb. Then, on May 18, 1970, he arrived at Valley Forge General Hospital near Phoenixville, Pennsylvania. Most of his other wounds had healed, but despite repeated surgeries, his foot was not getting better. In December 1970, Franks met with Dr. Phil Deffer, the chief of orthopedics to discuss his options.

Dr. Deffer told him two options were available. The first was continued surgery to eliminate the chronic infection in the stump of the foot that remained. The second was amputation. Even then there would be no guarantee that all the infection would be eliminated.

For Franks, a West Point graduate who had chosen to make the Army his career, his next question came quickly. "What about staying in the Army?" he asked.

"There's no way to do that and keep your leg," Dr. Deffer told him. "The Army does allow amputees to remain on active duty. But that depends on your motivation and the medical board recommendation."

Over Christmas 1970 Franks with his wife Denise mulled over what to do. Then in early January 1971, he told Dr. Deffer, "I want you to amputate my leg."

The amputation was performed later that month and was successful. The infection was gone. Transferred to the hospital's amputee ward, physical recovery came quickly, with Franks' body growing stronger and healthier with each passing day. The psychological recovery came much slower. Franks was not only emotionally affected by the loss of his limb, but also by the way the Vietnam War ended, and how poorly America, particularly its leaders, was treating veterans of the war, especially ones who had been seriously wounded. He later wrote, "The leaders abandoned the warriors. I could never forgive that betrayal of trust." As the days passed, a resolve formed out of rage began to grow within him. He later wrote, "Though I was helpless to make up for the absence of senior leaders, as the months went by, I grew ever more determined to do something more for those soldiers than [what] they were getting. . . . For all of my own personal loss, I knew-after the amputation-that I was going to be just fine. . . . And so there was lit what I . . . call the 'Hot Blue Flame.' I had a burning resolve to do what I could, in whatever my circle of responsibility, to see to it that soldiers never again found themselves in a situation where trust was fractured."

Once Franks made that commitment, he began the therapy to allow him to continue his career. The medical board cleared him for active duty. His dedication and commitment reached its pinnacle when he returned to combat as the commander of the VII Corps in Operations Desert Shield/Desert Storm and destroyed Iraq's Republican Guard.

A wounded Major Franks being carried to a medevac helicopter.
(James P. Sterba)

IF YOU'D LIKE TO DISCOVER MORE

During this period, the United States became the greatest power in the world. There are many excellent books that tell the story of the wars in this period. Here are just a few suggestions:

Remembering Korea by Jennifer Ashabranner
Colin Powell by Warren Brown
Ten Thousand Days of Thunder: A History of the Vietnam War by Philip Caputo
Congressional Medal of Honor Recipients by Kieran Doherty
The Causes of World War II by Paul Dowswell
American Women of the Vietnam War by Amanda Ferguson
Without Regard to Race: The Integration of the U.S. Military After World War II by Hedda Garza
The Tuskegee Airmen Story by Lynn M. Homen
Angels of Mercy: The Army Nurses of World War II by Betsy Khun
Red-Tail Angels: The Story of the Tuskegee Airmen of World War II by Pat McKissack
The Cold War by R. Conrad Stein
The Korean War: "The Forgotten War" by R. Conrad Stein

BIBLIOGRAPHY

Adams-Ender, Clara, Brigadier General, USA (Ret.) with Walker, Blair S. *My Rise to the Stars.* Lake Ridge, VA. CAPE. 2001.

Ambrose, Stephen E. *Crazy Horse and Custer.* New York. Anchor Books. 1996.

Astor, Gerald. *The Right to Fight.* Cambridge, MA. Da Capo Press. 1998.

Bauer, K. Jack. *The Mexican War 1846-1848.* Lincoln, Nebraska. Bison Books. 1974.

Bland, Larry I. Editor. *The Papers of George Catlett Marshall, Volumes 2 and 3.* Baltimore, MD. The Johns Hopkins University Press. 1986 and 1991.

Blumenson, Martin. *The Patton Papers 1885-1940.* New York. Da Capo Press. 1998.

Boatner III, Mark M. *The Biographical Dictionary of World War II.* Novato, CA. Presidio Press. 1996.

The Civil War Dictionary. New York. Vintage Books. 1988.

Buckley, Gail. *American Patriots.* New York. Random House. 2001.

Chambers II, John Whiteclay, Editor. *The Oxford Companion to American Military History.* New York. Oxford University Press. 1999.

Clancy, Tom, with Franks, General Fred, Jr. USA (Ret.). *Into the Storm.* New York. G. P. Putnam's Sons. 1997.

Copp, DeWitt S. *A Few Great Captains.* Garden City. Doubleday & Company. 1980.

Davis, Benjamin O., Jr. *Benjamin O. Davis, Jr. An Autobiography.* Washington, D.C., Smithsonian Institution Press. 1991.

Davis, Burke. *Marine! The Life of Chesty Puller.* New York. Bantam Books. 1988.

Dear, I.C.B., Editor. *The Oxford Companion to World War II.* New York. Oxford University Press. 1995.

D'Este, Carlo. *Patton A Genius for War.* New York. HarperCollins. 1995.

Dryden, Lt. Colonel Charles W. USAF (Ret.). *A-Train: Memoirs of a Tuskegee Airman.* Tuscaloosa, AL. The University of Alabama Press. 1997.

Dupuy, Trevor N.; Johnson, Curt; Bongard, David L. *The Harper Encyclopedia of Military Biography.* Edison, NJ. Castle Books. 1995.

Eisenhower, Dwight D. *At Ease: Stories I Tell to Friends.* Garden City. Doubleday & Company, Inc. 1967.

Eisenhower, John S. D. *Agent of Destiny: the Life and Times of General Winfield Scott.* Norman, Oklahoma. University of Oklahoma Press. 1997.

Ferling, John E., *The First of Men: A Life of George Washington.* Knoxville. The University of Tennessee Press. 1988.

Ferrell, Robert H., Editor. *The Eisenhower Diaries.* New York. W. W. Norton & Company. 1981.

Fletcher, Marvin E. *America's First Black General.* Lawrence. University of Kansas Press. 1989.

Flexner, James Thomas. *George Washington The Forge of Experience (1732-1775).* Boston. Little, Brown and Company. 1965.

Francis, Charles E. and Caso, Adolph. *The Tuskegee Airmen: The Men Who Changed a Nation.* Boston. Branden Publishing Co. 2002.

Glines, Colonel Carroll V., USAF. *The Saga of the Air Mail.* Princeton. D. Van Nostrand Company. 1968.

Grant, Ulysses S. *The Personal Memoirs of Ulysses S. Grant.* Old Saybrook, CT. Konecky & Konecky. 1992.

Hitsman, J. Mackay. *The Incredible War of 1812.* Toronto. Robrin Brass Studio.1999.

Hoffman, Colonel Jon T., USMCR. *Chesty: The Story of Lieutenant General Lewis B. Puller, USMC.* New York. Random House. 2001.

Holm, Jeanne, Major General USAF (Ret.). *Women in the Military: An Unfinished Revolution (Revised Edition).* Novato. Presidio Press. 1993.

James, D. Clayton. *The Years of MacArthur Volume 1 1880-1941.* Boston. Houghton Mifflin Company. 1970.

James, Marquis. *The Life of Andrew Jackson.* New York. The Bobbs-Merrill Company. 1938.

Johnson, Thomas H. *The Oxford Companion to American History.* New York. Oxford University Press. 1966.

Kinsley, D.A. *Custer: Favor the Bold.* New York. Promontory Press. 1968.

Krulak, Victor H. *First to Fight.* Annapolis. Naval Institute Press. 1984.

Leckie, Robert. *"A Few Acres of Snow" The Saga of the French and Indian Wars.* New York. John Wiley & Sons, Inc. 1999.

MacMillan, Margaret. *Paris 1919.* New York. Random House. 2001.

Manchester, William. *American Caesar.* New York. Dell. 1983.

Mee, Charles L., Jr. *End of Order Versailles 1919.* New York. Dutton. 1980.

Miller, Merle. *Ike The Soldier: As They Knew Him.* New York. G. P. Putnam's Sons. 1987.

Mosley, Leonard. *Marshall: Hero for Our Times.* New York. Hearst Books. 1982.

Murphy, Jack. *History of the U.S. Marines.* North Dighton, MA, World Publications Group, Inc. 2002.

O'Connor, Richard. *Black Jack Pershing.* Garden City. Doubleday & Company, Inc. 1961.

Ossad, Steven L., and Marsh, Don R. *Major General Maurice Rose.* Lanham, Maryland. Taylor Trade Publishing. 2003.

O'Toole. G.J.A. *The Spanish War: An American Epic 1898.* New York. W. W. Norton and Company. 1984.

Patton, Robert H. *The Pattons.* Washington, D.C. Brassey's. 1994.

Perrett, Bryon. *Impossible Victories.* New York. Barnes & Noble Books. 1996.

Pogue, Forrest C. *George Marshall Education of a General 1880-1939.* New York. The Viking Press. 1963.

Powell, Colin, with Persico, Joseph E. *My American Journey.* New York. Ballantine Books. 1996

Smith, Gene. *Lee and Grant.* New York. Meridian. 1984.

Sobel, Brian M. *The Fighting Pattons.* New York. Dell. 2000.

Socha, Rudy and Darrow, Carolyn. *Above & Beyond: former Marines Conquer the Civilian World.* Kentucky. Turner Publishing Company. 2003.

Symonds, Craig L. *American Heritage History of the Battle of Gettysburg.* New York. HarperCollins. 2001.

Tucker, Spencer C. Editor. *The Encyclopedia of the Vietnam War.* New York. Oxford University Press. 2000.

INTERVIEWS

Adams-Ender, Clara: Interview with author. November 18, 2003.
Mutter, Carol: Interview with author. December 17, 2003.
Vaught, Wilma: Interview with author. December 18, 2003.
Yeager, Charles: Interview with author. December 7, 2003.

SELECTED WEB SITES

There are many fine sites on the Internet dedicated to telling the stories of the military history of the United States and of the men and women who served in America's armed forces. Below is a small selection of useful websites:

THE LIBRARY OF CONGRESS
http://www.loc.gov
The American Memory website within the Library of Congress website is an exciting place filled with a wealth of historical information and illustrations.
THE NATIONAL ARCHIVES
http://www.archives.gov
The National Archives is the country's national record-keeper. It contains America's most important documents, which include the Declaration of Independence and the Constitution. It contains hundreds of thousands of digital records, photographs, and illustrations and is linked to all the presidential libraries.
THE NATIONAL MUSEUM OF AMERICAN JEWISH MILITARY HISTORY
www.nmajmh.org/index.html
The museum documents and preserves the contributions of Jewish Americans to the peace and freedom of the United States.

U.S. ARMY MILITARY HISTORY INSTITUTE
http://carlisle-www.army.mil/usamhi/
The official website for the Institute of the Army Heritage and Education Center is devoted to the preservation and distribution of the U.S. Army's heritage and history. It also has many useful links to other military websites.
UNITED STATES MARINE CORPS
http://www.usmc.mil
The official website of the U.S. Marine Corps. It contains links to Marine Corps history.
WOMEN MARINES ASSOCIATION
http://www.womenmarinies.org
The official website of the Women Marines Association, it contains a history of women in the Marines, biographies, milestone events, photographs, and other important information.
HISPANIC AMERICAN ARMY AIR FORCES HEROES OF WORLD WAR II
http://www.aetc.randolph.af.mil/ho/hispanic/hispanic_ww2.htm
This website is dedicated to telling the story of the contribution of Hispanic Americans in World War II
TUSKEGEE AIRMEN INC.
http://tuskegeeairmen.org
The official website of the Tuskegee Airmen is dedicated to the preservation of the legacy of the Tuskegee Airmen. The organization also provides scholarships to deserving high school students.
WOMEN IN MILITARY SERVICE FOR AMERICA MEMORIAL FOUNDATION, INC. (WIMSA)
www.womensmemorial.org
WIMSA is dedicated to preserving and presenting the history of women's contribution to America's military services.
CHUCKYEAGER.COM
http://www.chuckyeager.com
The official website for General Chuck Yeager and of aviation history. It is also the official website for the General Chuck Yeager Foundation that provides educational programs and scholarships to students.
DWIGHT D. EISENHOWER LIBRARY
http://www.eisenhower.archives.gov
The Eisenhower Library is the national repository for the Eisenhower papers and artifacts.
GEORGE C. MARSHALL FOUNDATION
http://www.marshallfoundation.org
The main repository for the collection of George Marshall papers. This site covers Marshall's contribution to the military and diplomatic history of the United States.
PATTON MUSEUM OF CAVALRY & ARMOR
http://www.generalpatton.org
This site is dedicated to telling the story of mechanized cavalry and armor.

INDEX

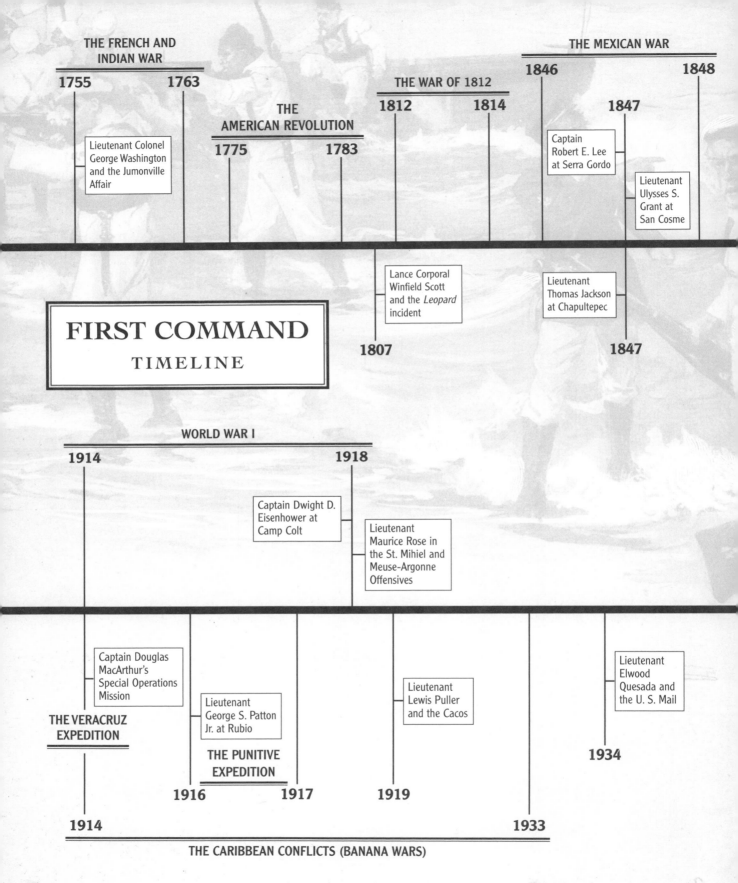

THE FRENCH AND
INDIAN WAR

1755 **1763**

THE MEXICAN WAR

1846 **1848**

THE WAR OF 1812

1812 **1814**

1847

THE
AMERICAN REVOLUTION

1775 **1783**

Lieutenant Colonel
George Washington
and the Jumonville
Affair

Captain
Robert E. Lee
at Serra Gordo

Lieutenant
Ulysses S.
Grant at
San Cosme

Lance Corporal
Winfield Scott
and the *Leopard*
incident

Lieutenant
Thomas Jackson
at Chapultepec

1807 **1847**

FIRST COMMAND
TIMELINE

WORLD WAR I

1914 **1918**

Captain Dwight D.
Eisenhower at
Camp Colt

Lieutenant
Maurice Rose in
the St. Mihiel and
Meuse-Argonne
Offensives

Captain Douglas
MacArthur's
Special Operations
Mission

Lieutenant
Elwood
Quesada and
the U. S. Mail

Lieutenant
George S. Patton
Jr. at Rubio

Lieutenant
Lewis Puller
and the Cacos

THE VERACRUZ
EXPEDITION

THE PUNITIVE
EXPEDITION

1916 **1917** **1919** **1934**

1914 **1933**

THE CARIBBEAN CONFLICTS (BANANA WARS)